ECHOES OF RESILIENCE

ECHOES OF RESILIENCE

A Tale of Two Grandmothers

Autobiographical Sketches by

Gertrude Jacobson Hult

Gertrud Beer Trobisch

Edited and translated by their grandson

David Trobisch

Quiet Waters Publications
2023

Quiet Waters Publications
Springfield, Missouri
www.quietwaterspub.com

Cover:
Gertrud Beer Trobisch (left), Gertrude Jacobson Hult (right)

International Distribution by Amazon
>US >UK >DE >FR >ES >IT >NL >PL >SE >JP >CA >AU

ISBN 978-1-931475-90-7

PREFACE

Mutti, pronounced with an 'oo' as in 'foot,' is my paternal grandmother from Leipzig, Germany. Mamita, on the other hand, is my maternal grandmother of Swedish-American descent. Both were born as the 19th century drew to a close.

Their lives unfold amid the tumultuous backdrop of two World Wars when their nations were locked in bitter conflict. Their memoirs shed light on the intricate dynamics of a family spanning international borders: Mamita's husband is driven by a divine calling to African missions. Mutti's son, a former soldier in Hitler's army, falls in love with Mamita's daughter.

Mamita and Mutti's narratives conclude before they meet for the first time at their children's wedding. Throughout their remarkable journeys, they embody courage and resilience as they navigate societal norms and constraints, ultimately shaping their family's future amidst challenging circumstances.

David Trobisch

CONTENT

Preface	5
The Ancestors (1850-1903)	8
Childhood and Education (1904-1918)	34
Marriage (1918-1922)	82
Motherhood (1923-1927)	122
Raising a Family (1927-1939)	136
World War II (1940-1945)	150
Epilogue	193
Table of Documents	204
Bibliography	206
Maps	207

THE ANCESTORS (1850-1903)

Miss Gertrude L. Jacobson

Parents

I was born on January 9, 1899, in the little coal-mining town of Sherrard, Illinois, to Gustaf Julius Jacobson and Albertina Stohl Jacobson. While my father was born in Varmland, Sweden, and immigrated to the U.S.A. with his mother and siblings, my mother was born on a farm in Grundy County, some 60 miles from Chicago.

Father came to the United States with his mother and five siblings. His father had preceded them by a couple of years and sent money twice for their passage to America. Unfortunately, he was cheated out of his money the first time. When they arrived at the port in Sweden ready to travel, they were informed there were no tickets. As a result, they had to return home and live with relatives for several months. Grandpa, who was working in a coal mine near Kewanee, Illinois, finally earned enough for them to travel to America. Father recalls two things about his ocean voyage - wearing a leather apron and copper-toed shoes and being teased by the sailors about them.

Father only attended school for about three years before being taken to work in the mine by his father at the age of 12. His job was to drive mules that pulled the coal carts. However, child labor was soon banned in Illinois, which meant he had to return to school until he was 14. Around this time, his parents moved to a farm near Geneseo in the same county, where they became members of the Swedish Lutheran Church, and Father was confirmed.

When my mother was an adult, her parents relocated to Cleveland, Illinois, approximately 12 miles from Geneseo. Her father passed away soon after at the age of 50. He is believed to have died of appendicitis, although the illness was not yet recognized then. Mother had more educational opportunities than Father did. She attended school for nine years and later worked as a teacher. In addition, she completed a dressmaker's course.

After Father and Mother married in 1888, they settled in various small coal-mining towns in the Illinois coal area where Father worked as a miner. Their three oldest sons were ten, eight, and four when I was born. Father's job later shifted to above ground at the mines as he became a weigh master. As time passed, my parents realized that a small coal-mining town was not ideal for raising children. Thus, they saved enough money to make a down payment on a 120-acre farm in Henry County. The farm was just two miles from my maternal grandmother's farm and about three or four miles from my Father's folks. It was a wise decision, as I was less than two months old when we moved there, and it provided a better environment for us children to grow up in.

As a child, I enjoyed a lot of freedom, and one incident stands out. I had wandered to the barn, where my father was cutting corn stalks with a rotary cutter and a team of horses attached. Waiting for him near the end of the row, I lay down and went to sleep. I was just in the path of the oncoming team, but as they neared me, the horses saw me and shied. Thankfully, my father found me and immediately took me to my mother.

Despite being poor by some standards, we had a good life on the farm. Father raised hogs, and we had several milk cows and a flock of hens. Butter and eggs were the currency that paid for our groceries, and I spent many hours churning butter in the old barrel. Our taxes, payments on the farm, clothing, and other necessities were often delayed until we had hogs to sell. But my parents were resourceful and thrifty, and my Mother was an excellent cook who always made sure we had plenty to eat. She carefully prepared our meals to avoid wasting food, ensuring there was barely enough to feed the cats and dog.

We planted gardens and canned fruits and vegetables every year for the winter. We studied nursery catalogs and ordered new fruit or shade trees, vines, or plants. Once, we even planted a pear orchard of 100 trees, some of which still survive and bear fruit. We had patches of strawberries, raspberries, plums of various kinds, blackberries, apples, peaches, and cherries, though the frost would sometimes kill the blossoms. We also had gooseberries, currants, and rhubarb.

After school, we would change into our work clothes and eat fruit from the trees and bushes around the farm. In the winter, there were bins of potatoes and apples in our cellar, jars of salt pork or fried-down pork, smoked hams on the rafters, barrels of cider which later became vinegar and was also sold, jars of lard, canned fruit, and vegetables. Before bedtime on winter evenings, someone would go down to the cellar and bring apples to eat or pop some corn.

We spent our winter evenings reading, playing games like dominoes, checkers, flinch, pit, carom, and more, or listening to someone play the organ or piano. Father often played his violin and asked one of his daughters to accompany him.

I began attending the nearby rural school when I was five, turning six in January. I enjoyed school and was in good health, so I never missed a day in the eight years I attended the little white schoolhouse. Fortunately, we stayed in the same place throughout that time, and my mother ensured I always arrived on time and never had to stay home to help with chores. My brother and I would milk the cows before breakfast, help with the dishes, and then Mother would braid my hair before we set off for school with our lunches. We rarely went home for lunch. Instead, we ate the mid-day meal at school. We lived half a mile from the school, and Mother always saw that we were on time.

Our school had around 25 children from eight grades with only one teacher. We had great fun playing at recess and noon, engaging in various games that country school children knew, such as blackman, darebase, last couple out, andy over, baseball, fox and geese, and sled riding. When the weather was bad, we played catch in the hall with a ball or blackboard games. I always ran to school when the roads were good, and one teacher told me later that she always knew when I was coming because I always ran. This probably explains why I became a fast runner and outpaced anyone my size, whether boy or girl. I eagerly looked forward to summer holiday picnics, Fourth of July celebrations, and Farmers' picnics because there were always running races for the children, and I won every race I ever entered. The prizes, such as shoes, a rocking chair, a carpet sweeper, or a looking glass, were sometimes very good.

I loved school and studying and was never content unless I was first in my class, although there were never more than three or four in my grades. Our teachers were mostly women, except for one year when we had a male teacher. There would be a box supper once during the year, and there were programs for parents at various times. The last day of school, picnic was a memorable event when our parents would come, and we had a big feast.

Throughout grade school, I always had a sibling there with me, and one year, we had three siblings attending the same school.

At the age of nine, I began taking lessons on our parlor organ. My father bought a piano the following year, and I continued taking piano lessons every summer after that. My father played the violin and taught me how to chord so I could accompany him. As I learned to read notes, we enjoyed playing music together, although I never became a skilled musician.

COAL MINING IN ILLINOIS (1867)

"Grandpa, who was working in a coal mine near Kewanee, Illinois, finally earned enough for them (his wife and the five children) to travel to America." (Mamita)

Kewanee, Illinois

1867 – The mining of coal was a major asset for the early economy of Kewanee. In 1867 a state geological report asserted that 53,000 tons of coal were mined in and around Kewanee; 32,000 tons of which were shipped, 14,000 tons used by the railroad and the rest used for home consumption. There were many small mines; but according to the report Platt Coal Co. was the largest, embracing about 1,000 acres of land, and "by some arrangement handles and markets all the coal mined in the vicinity." The report concluded that "the revenue derived from this deposit of mineral wealth will build Kewanee into a place of consequence." Lathrop Coal Co., founded in 1869, was also a major producer, employing about 200 miners. There would be more than 100 mines, many of them small operations. Most mines were "drift" mines dug into the side of a hill or ravine, but some were shaft mines. [...] Coal mining would continue to be an important business around Kewanee until the 1930's. The last mine closed in 1946.

> *Excerpt from: Larry Lock, "KEWANEE—1854-2004" Family Histories of Henry County (Henry County Genealogical Society: Kewanee, 2000). The author was president of the Kewanee Historical Society and curator of its Robert and Marcella Richards Museum.*

Sherrard, Illinois

> *"I was born on January 9, 1899, in the little coal-mining town of Sherrard, Illinois. … As time passed, my parents realized that a small coal-mining town was not ideal for raising children." (Mamita)*

David Sherrard, the man whom Sherrard Village was named after, was born February 1, 1818. The Sherrards came to Mercer County Illinois in 1854. David Sherrard planned and plotted the town. The first lots were sold in May of 1894 and by January 1, 1895 there were fifty houses and nearly all of them were occupied by miners and their families.

David Sherrard was president of the first bank of Sherrard in 1896. He was also in the order of DeMolay. It is a Character Building 0rganization for Young Men, from 13-21 and is a part of the Masonic Lodge. David Sherrard was a member of its first advisory council.

> *Excerpt from a typoscript found in the Sherrard Public Library. Tammy Wilson. Senior. Illinois History. May 1982.*

Mamita

Before the season of 1894, a large amount of prospecting for coal was done in Sherrard by the Coal Valley Mining Company. They found a good vein of coal covering several hundred acres of territory.

The actual sinking of the mine took place on March 13, 1894, when the first boiler and steam engine was hauled from Preemption by a team of horses, as the railroad had not been laid out from that place to Sherrard. The shaft was the opening from the surface to the vein of coal from below. The size of the shaft was 16 feet square, and four elevators were hung in it. The sinking of the hole was difficult as the water flowed freely after they had reached a depth of 30 feet and had to be pumped out in order to allow the men to dig and blast out the rock.

The coal seam was reached on July 10 when the first boxes of coal were lifted out. They found it was not the main vein, so the sinking was continued till August 16, when the full depth was reached.

The miners loaded the cars with coal, and boys with mules pulled it to the main roads, where cable trains picked it up, and hauled it to the shaft bottom, where it was then put in elevator cages and hauled to the top.

An average of 300 men were employed at the mine and occasionally when there was more work, as many as 400 were employed! The daily output of the mine was 725 tons, and, on some days, it exceeded 1000 tons! This was dangerous work and the sound of the mine whistle blowing at odd times of the day, denoting an emergency, struck fear in the citizens of Sherrard.

The ups and downs of the population were mainly because of the mines. The population of 1875 was 365. In the year 1900, the federal census stated a population of 906. By 1920, however, the population was at a record low of 327. This loss of almost 2/3 of the

Mamita

population was due to the mines closing, which forced them to look for jobs elsewhere.

Excerpt from a typoscript found in the Sherrard Public Library. Moly DePorter. Junior. Illinois History. May 1982.

[Philip M. Minneci, History Teacher at Sherrard High School, noted that the articles were researched and written by Sherrard High students who were enrolled in the 'Illinois History' class.]

Fräulein A. Gertrud Beer

Paternal Grandparents

In the heart of Germany, in the Thuringian region, on both banks of the Saale river, not far from the famous Rudelsburg castle, lies the town of Camburg. Around the middle of the 19th century, my grandfather Christian Beer lived and worked here as a school director with his wife and seven children: three daughters and four sons. The daughters, according to the custom of the time, had no profession, and two of them remained unmarried.

The oldest daughter left her parents when her oldest brother lost his wife. She cared for his household and two small children and stayed with him until her death. The youngest daughter moved away when she married. Auguste, the third daughter, initially helped her mother and then cared for her father after her mother's death. When he also passed away around 1900, she continued living in the schoolhouse and taught handicraft lessons.

Auguste was always present when we visited our grandfather or, after his death, visited the family home. Naturally, my memories of Camburg are associated with her. Auguste had a good heart and always aimed to bring us joy. She often took us hiking to the Rudelsburg castle. However, for us children, she was the epitome of a pedantic, somewhat rigid old maid. Even as adults, we still looked up to her with fearful respect.

This was not just the case with her nieces and nephews. My mother, who came from a wealthy family and grew up in the city, often told the story of her first visit to Camburg as a bride. At every celebration in the Saale town, traditional Thuringian dumplings, made from raw potatoes, were served for lunch. My mother had never eaten such dumplings before and struggled to eat the fist-sized lump. Just as she took a relieved breath, another dumpling appeared on her plate. She was almost desperate, and it is telling of the atmosphere around Aunt Auguste that the young bride didn't dare to say anything and struggled to swallow the second dumpling.

The more I think about the prank my younger brother Rudi played when he was about two years old, the more I smile. We were visiting Camburg and had finished dinner, and Aunt Auguste's strict eyes scanned the table. She spotted a small leftover piece of butter and said in an accusing tone, "Well, this tiny bit of butter didn't need to be left over!" In a flash, Rudi climbed onto his chair, reached out his little hand, grabbed the piece of butter, and happily ate it with his fingers. Aunt Auguste froze like a statue!

Another incident from Camburg has left a lasting impression on me. It was during our vacation there when my older sister Mariechen and I, both aged eleven and twelve, found ourselves in a tight spot. Our Aunt Auguste, who resided in the school building, had prepared a scrumptious cherry tart before heading downstairs to teach her class.

Now, Aunt Auguste entrusted us with the important task of delivering the pastry to the local baker for baking. But before we embarked on this mission, she made sure we diligently swept the entire apartment and meticulously dusted every nook and cranny, sparing no leaf on her precious potted plants.

As soon as Aunt Auguste left, Mariechen and I sprang into action. Within a mere ten minutes, we completed all the chores and excitedly ventured out of the house. After dutifully delivering the tart to the baker, the warm rays of the sun lured us into taking a leisurely stroll through the enchanting Saale river valley. Oh, the temptation was simply irresistible to us, two young city dwellers!

Little did we know that Aunt Auguste had forgotten something and sent a schoolchild to retrieve it, assuming we would still be at home. But, oh no! We were nowhere to be seen.

Aunt Auguste was utterly shocked by our audacious act, and it took her months to recover. The very idea of us daring to take a leisurely stroll while others diligently toiled away was simply scandalous! Oh, the sheer frivolity of it all!

Poor Aunt Auguste! She suffered a broken hip at the age of eighty. It is a dear memory that I could visit her at the hospital and bring her fresh fruit from our garden. Shortly after her return home, Aunt passed away around the year 1940. I am still grateful to her today for having stored so many potatoes, which I could bring to Leipzig for my hungry family when we dissolved Aunt's household.

The Beer family had four sons, each of whom pursued different careers. Adolf, the eldest, became a machine fitter, Carl trained as a teacher for the deaf and dumb, Gustav studied theology, and Rudolf, who was my father and born on March 23, 1853, attended the University of Leipzig to study Latin, Greek, Hebrew, and German as a classical philologist.

My dad had a keen interest in the German language and had high standards for it. Long after he passed away, I discovered a collection of articles he had published. Although mostly book reviews, the articles all related to language and speech training in some way. He was especially critical of linguistic mistakes and errors and had a humorous way of pointing them out.

Once, he went too far in his criticism of the extravagant lifestyles of military officers during maneuvers and was punished with eight days of house arrest. To his surprise, he enjoyed the punishment as it gave him an excuse not to leave the house.

My father regarded foreign words as the biggest threat to the purity of the German language and passionately fought against their use. He did not allow any foreign words to be used in his home.

Since my father had paid for his own education, he jumped at every opportunity to earn money. He taught at a private school, read to a blind person, and wrote articles for the newspaper. After completing his studies in 1876, he became a Doctor of Philosophy and began teaching at the Thomasschule, a classical gymnasium in Leipzig. After a few years, he became a "Professor." However, he never placed much importance on this title and always referred to himself as "Doktor Beer" because he "had truly earned the doctorate."

On our front door was a white sign with black letters that read "Dr. Rudolf Beer."

Father's Marriage

Due to his desire to pay off all of his debts first, Father married very late in life. He married Gertrud Anna Pfitzer, who used her middle name, Anna, in March of 1890 at the age of 37. Anna was 15 years younger than him and the only daughter of a wealthy factory owner. More than half a century later, I cannot say much about my parents' marriage. However, music brought them together and strengthened their bond over time. Both were highly skilled and passionate musicians. Father played the piano exceptionally well, both by sight and by heart. He enjoyed accompanying his young wife's bright soprano and would often join in with his sonorous bass, which I still remember.

My parents often played music together outside of the home at social events and charity functions. They also enjoyed listening to good music, often attending concerts and visiting the Motette at the Thomaskirche on Saturdays to hear the singing of the Thomaner choir. At orchestral concerts, they always brought a score with them so they could follow the music closely.

Siblings

On January 31, 1891, the oldest daughter Hertha was born. On June 18, 1892, the second daughter, Hedwig Marie, was born, and on June 2, 1893, I was born and given the same names as my mother but in reverse order, Anna Gertrud.

According to my mother's stories, my birth brought more disappointment than joy. I was the third child born within 28 months, the third girl and a tiny baby weighing only four and a half pounds, although fully developed and carried to term! The woman who lived above us had just bought her Sunday roast. She is said to have weighed it in both hands and said, "That's exactly the size of the baby!"

I must have cried a lot. My mother often told me that my sister Marie, who was only slightly older and had an extremely gentle nature throughout her life, would slide over to my cradle and soothe me by rocking me back and forth while singing "Tralala."

Frailty accompanied me throughout my childhood. If there were an illness anywhere, I would catch it. I lost all my baby teeth very early, and it took years for the other teeth to come in. I remember my father peeling plums for me because my mother didn't have the patience or time to do it. On November 3, 1895, the long-awaited son Rudolf was born, and six years later, on October 31, 1901, our youngest, Irmgard Helene, was born.

One of the illnesses that stands out from my childhood memories is scarlet fever, which I contracted in the first grade when I was seven. As neither my father nor my sisters were permitted to attend school during my illness, I had to be isolated and sent to a children's hospital. When I was picked up by an ambulance, Rudi watched from the window, fascinated by the "rubber carriage" and wishing he could ride in such a vehicle. Rudi also developed scarlet fever two weeks later and was transported to the hospital in a "rubber carriage."

I was too sick to care about anything then, and I spent the first three weeks with a high fever, always with an ice pack on my chest. Even though my brother was in the next bed, it didn't mean anything to me, except that his teasing bothered me. My condition gradually improved over the following weeks, and I began participating in all the pranks devised in the dormitory with around 40 other children.

One memory that has stuck with me is of a morning when the chief doctor came for his rounds, and we were all sitting on our chamber pots in bed, singing loudly: "We are the children of the scarlet fever house. We live and die for singing!"

During our illness, my parents spent a very anxious night. They saw a huge fire in the east of the city, where the children's hospital was located. They hurried there and discovered that the large Riebeck brewery, right next to the hospital, was burning brightly. When they were told that all the nurses were on standby and all the stretchers and sick beds were ready, they could return home reassured. During their visits, they were only allowed to see us through a glass door.

During my illness, my grandfather in Leipzig passed away and was buried. I am unsure if the mourners came straight from the cemetery to the hospital. However, I still vividly remember the black figures and tearful faces, which deeply moved me and stayed in my mind for days.

When I think about my return after six weeks in the hospital, I still feel the disappointment I felt then. By then, the summer vacation had already started, and my father had taken my two sisters and Rudi, who had been discharged before me, to the summer resort in Diesbar an der Elbe that had been rented long before. It was a heavy blow for me! It didn't matter that my mother was at home, and the new large doll carriage didn't give me any comfort, as I had to take my doll for a walk alone in the yard.

I was only happy again when we were all reunited in Diesbar. I still regret not being allowed to go into the water. Scarlet fever left me with a memory that lasted for over four decades. During that time, my second set of teeth formed and appeared with large "dents" that were always a welcome feast for bacteria.

I know that my father contributed a lot to the embellishment of wedding celebrations. Both parents sang at the church wedding. Father often wrote a humorous table song, gave one of his witty speeches, and otherwise contributed to the entertainment of the guests. He was a good companion.

We children were also expected to contribute to the entertainment with our singing. As both parents had a large circle of friends and Mother's friends got married after her, we were often invited to be flower girls. It was certainly not easy to dress four small children in floral garlands. One day, however, when the flower-decorated wedding carriage was already waiting in front of the house to pick us up, three-year-old Rudi could not be found; in his white suit, he sat happily playing with briquettes in the coal bin. - There was another great fun at this wedding. We all stood at the table opposite the bride and groom and sang our little song. But Rudi didn't sing along. He carefully lifted the long white tablecloth and examined where people had their legs.

Reflecting on the first ten years of my childhood, I recall a harmonious family life in a comfortable middle-class setting. We always had a maid to take care of the household, and we went on summer vacations every year, mostly to Manebach in the Thuringian Forest. We were there during the summer before Father's passing.

Father's Death

Like all young men who had served as "conscripts," my father remained with the military as a reserve officer after his term of service. That meant he had to participate in a training exercise every year. Being by nature small and delicate, he likely pushed himself too hard during these exercises, especially the unfamiliar horseback riding. In any case, a heart condition developed even before the turn of the century. That is why we moved 1900 from the apartment near the school to the Kronprinzstraße, about 35 minutes away, because the daily walk to school was supposed to strengthen his heart. It probably didn't help much. Even multiple visits to heart spas were unsuccessful.

Shortly after his 25th anniversary of service, for which his colleagues presented him with a bust of Goethe, our father passed away at the age of 50 on December 13, 1903. He had been bedridden for several weeks at home, cared for by a nurse who lived with us. My only memory of her is that she ate the sprats with the bones while we always carefully removed the pesky bones from these little smoked fish.

Father lay in bed in his study in the last days of his illness. Here he died, and here he was laid out. I snuck over to him several times a day and gently stroked his hands. Although I recoiled every time from the icy coldness, I soon felt irresistibly drawn back to the dear deceased. When I was caught once at his bier, the room was locked. But this early experience of death has still profoundly ingrained itself in my soul and left unforgettable impressions. We four older children – Irmgard was only two years old – then had to stay with the family all day, who lived below us and whose four sons were almost the same age as us. I felt this was a punishment for my behavior. But our brother

Rudi skillfully sneaked away several times daily to see his mama and caress her. I know from her account how much she appreciated this tenderness from her little son.

My father's funeral at the newly established Südfriedhof was imposing and must have lasted long. Two eulogies were given, one by Pastor Teichgräber from the Andreaskirche to which we belonged and the other by Uncle Gustav, the son of my paternal grandfather, followed by the obituaries of all the associations to which the deceased had belonged; I still remember the "Allgemeiner Deutscher Sprachverein" and the "Verein für Volkswohl." The singing of the Thomaner choir accompanied the ceremony.

For ten years after my father's death, the alums sang a moving song at his grave on the early morning of St. John's Day (June 24), the day of remembrance for the dead.

BROTHERS ERNST FRIEDRICH AND GOTTLOB HEINRICH PFITZER OF OSCHATZ (1845-1902)

"During my illness, my grandfather in Leipzig passed away and was buried. I am unsure if the mourners came straight from the cemetery to the hospital. However, I still vividly remember the black figures and tearful faces, which deeply moved me and stayed in my mind for days."
(Mutti's manuscript)

Ernst Friedrich Pfitzer was born on October 7, 1819, in Oschatz as the third son of the master cloth maker Gottlob Heinrich Pfitzer and his wife Christiana Friederica Grell, the daughter of the master sawyer Johann Heinrich Grell. The family included eight children, five sons and three daughters.

The Pfitzers were a long-established family of hardworking craftsmen and farmers in the Oschatz area. Even during his childhood, one could often find Ernst Friedrich Pfitzer with his brothers in the blacksmith's workshop of his grandfather Johann Heinrich Grell at the 'Altmarkt'. Even at 85, Grell was the master of the carpenter's, sawyer's and blacksmith's trades in Oschatz.

He inspired his five grandsons, but especially Ernst Friedrich, with a love for the blacksmith's trade and a striving for knowledge and skill.

Since the craft business also produced small beam scales, Ernst Friedrich first came into contact with scales here. So, it is not surprising that Ernst Friedrich Pfitzer, just like his brother Heinrich Reinhold [Mutti's biological grandfather] from 1838 to 1842, learned the trade of carpenter and sawyer from his uncle Johann Heinrich Grell, jun. in Meißen-Garsebach from 1837 to 1840, and

30

Mutti

on July 18, 1841, according to old guild tradition, was declared a free journeyman carpenter "before the assembled craftsmen".

Returning from his travels to his hometown of Oschatz, the 25-year-old Ernst Friedrich Pfitzer presented his masterpiece on April 12, 1845, and was declared a master of the carpenter's and sawyer's trades by the master of the guild. [...] Two days after becoming a master, namely on April 14, 1845, the carpenter and sawyer master Ernst Friedrich Pfitzer gained the citizenship rights of Oschatz. In the same month, on April 26, 1845, he publicly announced the foundation of the company "Ernst Friedrich Pfitzer – Zeugschmiede [Toolsmith]". As a company logo, Pfitzer used a lion, the coat of arms of Oschatz, which holds a beam scale in its paw. With a "P" for "Pfitzer" noted below it. [...]

In 1849, Pfitzer became the presiding master of the carpenters' and sawyers' guild (Obermeister der Zeug- und Sägeschmiedeinnung), where he had already been an assessor since 1846. For many years he was also the calibration master (Eichmeister) in Oschatz.

His craft business increasingly developed from a small tool forge to a factory. The demand for scales grew significantly during this time, which helped Pfitzer to a flourishing business.

Heinrich Reinhold Pfitzer [Mutti's grandfather], the brother of Ernst Friedrich Pfitzer, gained citizenship rights on August 5, 1853, joined the company as a partner in June 1855, and has been acting as owner since 1862. From then on, the company advertised under the name "Gebrüder Pfitzer, Waagen-Fabrik [Scale Factory], Oschatz i. S[achsen].". [...] With initially hardly a dozen workers, the company grew steadily. While between 1851 and 1862 a total of only 1,000 bridge scales were produced, the company produced 4,000 bridge scales alone in just nine months in 1862 - a huge increase in production. [...]

31

Mutti

In October 1874, Heinrich Reinhold Pfitzer left the company and committed suicide in 1876. Ernst Friedrich Pfitzer was from then on the sole owner of the company. From the marriage of Ernst Friedrich Pfitzer to his wife Amalia Friederica Fischer, two sons and seven daughters were born, of which both sons and two daughters died in early childhood. Therefore, Pfitzer had no male successor for his scale factory. When he took his daughter Emma Laura to the World Exhibition in Vienna in 1873, she met there the Austrian merchant Leopold Carl Bruck, who was experienced in the iron trade. Both married on July 5, 1875 in Oschatz. Since Bruck was a Jew and as such was not allowed to appear in Oschatz, he converted to Protestantism before the wedding. The couple had six sons and two daughters. A month after the wedding, Bruck joined his father-in-law's company as a proxy and was co-owner from January 7, 1881. [...]

At the age of 64, Ernst Friedrich Pfitzer retired, left the company on July 7, 1883, and handed over the flourishing company to his son-in-law Leopold Carl Bruck. With Bruck as the sole owner, the company henceforth bore the name "Gebrüder Pfitzer, Waagenfabrik [Scale Factory], Owner: Leopold Carl Bruck". [...]

The scale manufacturer Ernst Friedrich Pfitzer died on July 1, 1902 from a stroke. With his death, the heyday of the Oschatz scale factory founded in 1845 also ended. As a widower, he left behind four daughters who had to be provided for from the large inheritance.

> *Dana Bach, Manfred Schollmeyer (editors). Oschatzer Geschichten(n): Auf den Spuren berühmter Persönlichkeiten – Ernst Friedrich Pfitzer – Mitbegründer des industriellen Waagenbaus in Deutschland. (Oschatz: Oschatzer Geschichts- und Heimatverein e.V., 2019) Heft 13.*

[Excerps are translated from pages 6, 7, 10, 22, 27, 32. Ernst Friedrich Pfitzer is the "grandfather in Leipzig" who Mutti mentions in her

Mutti

manuscript. Her biological grandfather, however, was Ernst Friedrich's brother Heinrich Reinhold Pfitzer who committed suicide in 1876.]

CHILDHOOD AND EDUCATION
(1904-1918)

Miss Gertrude L. Jacobson

On the Farm

I believe I liked the work, as I can't remember rebel-ling against it, although I am sure I was often lazy and careless and had to be reminded by my parents. My sister and I often disagreed on how to wash and dry the dishes, but we were not punished very often. When we were, though, the memory of it lasted a long time. The punishment was always dealt justly, and it seemed to "keep us good." Only once do I remember being spanked by my father, and I can't remember why it happened, but I do remember the "how." It was with his razor strop. It must have worked, for I cannot remember another time he or my mother had to spank me. My mother's punishments were usually slaps, which were more easily forgotten and less feared.

We always had a dog and cats. The dog was usually part collie and a natural companion to us children. He was trained to go with us to the woods pasture after the cows and round them up, even when they were in the farthest corner. I remember playing with the cats and thinking, "I'd rather play with a kitty—something alive—than with the prettiest dolly."

Summer vacations were full of many things—both work and play. When the corn reached a certain stage, Father would have us children pull weeds every year. There were certain patches where the morning glories and smartweeds wanted to take over, and as an incentive, he would pay us a few cents for every row we cleared of weeds. This helped, as we were happy to have a little money to spend on the Fourth of July on ice cream cones and firecrackers. As a rule, we girls did nothing in the fields but helped in the garden and the house and kept the yard clean and mowed. In the afternoons, we were often free to read books, play with neighbor children, exchange visits, sew, embroider, or practice our piano lessons. I didn't learn much about cooking until high school when I took Home Economics and learned cooking and sewing. At that time, my mother encouraged me more in baking. I remember making my own wedding cakes, which were angel foods.

Father and Mother were not church members and seldom went to church themselves. However, they encouraged us to attend Sunday School regularly. We lived two miles away from a little Methodist church, and sometimes we walked there, but more often, we drove old Pete, our trustworthy white horse. We would blanket him during cold weather while he was tied to a hickory tree outside the church. I remember how fast he could travel, especially toward home. We often went to Grandma Stohl's house for dinner, and the folks would be there too. (That grandmother died when I was twelve.) Speaking of Pete, he was temperamental but not mean. The worst trouble we had was putting a bridle on him. Father or one of my brothers usually harnessed him, but sometimes the men would be in the fields, so it was up to us. He could raise his mouth so high that we had to climb on the manger to bridle him.

The doctor seldom visited us, but once, a horse kicked my brother Verne in the mouth. Father brought him unconscious, and I remember how shocked my mother and I were. The worst damage was the loss of a tooth and a cut lip that had to be sewn up.

I cannot remember being sick while I attended grade school. I had mumps and scarlet fever before starting school and measles in my second year of high school. That was the first school day I had missed in my life, and I was so unhappy to have my perfect attendance record broken. I have always been thankful for good health, then and even later.

When I was 13, I started high school at Geneseo High School, nine miles away from home, too far to walk back and forth each day. So, my neighbor girl and I found a place to stay in town from Monday morning until Friday evening. Our fathers would take turns meeting and taking us, or we could go by train from a station three miles from home. Once, just for fun, I walked home and did it in 2 hours and 15 minutes, getting there before my roommate and her father. I guess I ran a good part of the way. Little did I know it at the time, but I was conditioning myself for long walks in Africa—although none ever went that far that fast.

Education (1915-1916)

I thoroughly enjoyed my high school days because I genuinely loved learning. I was also quite active in sports, particularly girls' basketball and volleyball. In my last year, I even joined the girls' glee club. We played volleyball together as well. Thanks to my mother's persistent urging, I completed the four-year course in just three years. However, I've come to regret that decision in later years, as I lacked the necessary time I had to take some high school subjects while in college. So, at the age of 16 in 1915, I proudly graduated from high school. The following autumn, I enrolled as a student at Macomb Normal School. My mother, being a teacher herself, thought it was a suitable path for me to pursue. I attended for a full year and even a summer term. During the first two terms, I worked in the kitchen and dining room to earn my board and room.

While at Macomb Normal School, I had a significant spiritual experience—I became a Christian. I regularly attended YWCA meetings and the Methodist church, finding great spiritual nourishment and joy in my new-found faith and the fellowship of other young Christians. Although I had initially hoped to pursue a career in teaching after completing the teachers' training program, I encountered an obstacle. Illinois laws prohibited individuals under the age of 18 from teaching. It became clear that God had different plans for me.

A neighbor girl who was planning to attend Augustana College that year invited me to join her as her roommate. My parents agreed as the college was located in Rock Island, less than 20 miles from our home. Those three years at Augustana were truly transformative for me. I cherished the company of fellow Christians and reveled in the opportunity to study Bible, doctrine, church history, and other theological subjects. Before long, I decided to become a Lutheran. My decision was solidified as I witnessed Lutheranism in action, observing how it was practiced in daily life.

Courtship and Engagement (1917)

During my time at college, I formed deep Christian friendships. One particular friend, Anna Cesander, had a profound influence on me. We attended various religious gatherings together, including Sunday afternoon meetings of the Mission Society, Saturday evening prayer meetings with fellow students, Sunday morning Bible classes, and church services. Anna also introduced me to the Student Volunteer Band, a dedicated group of students passionate about missions. Remarkably, every member of that group went on to become a pastor or a missionary overseas. The band organized annual mission study classes, and in my first year, I joined the class focused on Islam, led by a missionary from India.

During the second semester of that year, I met Ralph Hult. He was a member of a gymnastic club that held an annual banquet accompanied by a public demonstration in the gymnasium. The class director kindly invited me as his guest, and I found myself seated between him and the college president. Little did I realize at the time, but the most significant event of the evening was when Anna introduced me to Ralph, who happened to be her banquet guest. Soon after, Ralph invited me to accompany him to one of the College Lyceum meetings held in the college chapel. That evening, a Denver juvenile court judge spoke about juvenile delinquency. I can't recall the details of his speech, but what stands out in my memory is the walk and conversation we had afterward.

Around that time, I was facing an important decision. Having just turned 18, my parents wanted me to join the Eastern Star lodge. My father had been a Mason since he was 21, and he and my mother had been members of the Eastern Stars for several years. I was unsure of what to do. When I shared my predicament with Ralph, he directed me to a Bible verse that has remained significant in our lives ever since—Psalm 32:8: "I will instruct thee and teach thee in the way which thou shalt go: I will guide thee with mine eye." God indeed provided me with guidance, and after much study and prayer, I decided not to join the lodge.

While I am grateful for that decision, knowing it was right, it was a difficult blow for my parents to accept. They accused me of becoming a fanatic. From that point on, it created a divide between us that remained throughout their lives. Neither they nor I changed our positions. Upon reflecting on it, I believe their dedication to the lodge became their form of religion. Regularly attending the lodge gatherings seemed to fulfill their spiritual needs. The ideals, morals, and teachings practiced within the lodge became their way of attaining righteousness. During this time, I had a conversation with my father, asking him, "If you were to die tomorrow, what would happen to you?" He responded immediately and confidently, "I believe I would go straight to heaven." He went on to recount his virtues. Although I acknowledged that he was a good man in the eyes of the world and that he had always been a loving husband and father, I couldn't agree that his righteousness alone would save him. It seemed that he felt no need for the Savior, who had become my life source.

After the Lyceum lecture on April 13th, Ralph and I started spending much time together. We went on many long walks and had meaningful conversations. It didn't take long for us to realize that we were in love, although we hadn't officially declared it to each other. I originally planned to teach at a country school the following year, but Ralph encouraged me to continue my studies at Augustana. I was uncertain about how to proceed. I tried to find summer employment and ended up working as a maid in a Rock Island home, where I would receive room and board and five dollars a week.

Then something unexpected happened. The Synod was scheduled to meet at Augustana College that year to commemorate the 400th anniversary of the Reformation. The matron in the girls' dormitory offered me work after school was out, cleaning the dormitory to prepare for the arrival of the Synodical guests. For two weeks, I diligently washed all the walls and woodwork in East Hall. I believe the building still stands and has served as Music Hall for many years. Several other students and I were assigned to help with feeding, serving tables, and washing dishes for the large crowd during the convention.

Around the time of my second date with Ralph, Anna warned me. She cautioned that if I continued my relationship with him, I would likely become a missionary in Africa. I had already learned about Ralph's interest in and personal calling to Sudan, Africa. The Augustana Missionary Society recommended to the Synod that they begin work in Sudan and appoint Ralph as their first missionary there. Many prayers were lifted up from Zion Hill that spring, asking God to open the door for our Synod to work in Sudan. While our Synod had missions in China, India, and Puerto Rico, it had none in Africa or South America. This became a burden of prayer for many students and some of the professors. Members of the Student Volunteer Band gathered on Zion Hill multiple times, with the birds singing above them and early spring flowers blooming at their feet. In a marvelous way, God answered those prayers.

During that time, the guests were being served in the old gym connected to the new one at the front. The kitchen was located in the new gym, close to where the front doors are now situated. I was aware that the Sudan proposition would be brought up for discussion on June 14th. I was granted a temporary break from my duties to attend the session. Standing on the platform of the new gym, Ralph addressed the delegates and friends gathered there (numbering several hundred) about the pressing needs of the people in Sudan for the message of Jesus. At that time, Sudan was one of the largest areas in the world without any presence of missionaries. The spread of Islam in North Africa was steadily advancing southward, posing a significant threat to the populous pagan communities of Africa. What was required was a chain of mission stations across Africa to halt the encroaching tide of Islam. Ralph also shared his personal calling to serve in Sudan. I listened attentively to the questions asked and answered and the ensuing discussions. Then the president called for a vote. I will never forget the resounding "Ja" (which means "yes" in Swedish, as the meeting was conducted in Swedish at that time) that echoed throughout the room as the vote was cast. The president declared, "It is unanimous. I am glad that it is unanimous."

On June 17th, Ralph was ordained for his calling to serve in Sudan. Then, on the evening of June 18th, a whole session of the Synod meeting was dedicated to Ralph's commissioning as their first missionary to Africa. Ralph's mother and I sat together during that meeting, our hearts filled with joy and gratitude. The night before, Ralph had asked me to be his bride, and I had happily accepted. His calling had become my own.

However, due to the ongoing war, there was no immediate possibility of us going to Africa. It was decided that Ralph would spend the following year at the Kennedy School of Missions in Hartford, Connecticut.

That autumn, he went to Hartford, and I returned to Augustana for my junior year of college. But before he left, Ralph wanted our engagement to be official.

He had already written to my parents, seeking their permission to marry me, and they had given their consent. On September 26th, we left Rock Island together to go to the farm. I still recall the delightful aroma that welcomed us as we opened the door—the scent of Mother frying apples. It was a moment I will never forget. As the meal ended, with only the four of us at the table, Ralph placed the ring on my finger.

The next day, we returned to Augustana. I was informed that in my absence, I had been chosen as the president of the Girls' Glee Club, called the Orioles. The club consisted of 24 members, and I sang with them for both of the following years.

The separation in the fall was not easy for us young lovers, as we were unsure how long it would last.

RALPH HULT AND GERTRUDE JACOBSON MEET (1917)

"During the second semester of that year [1917], I met Ralph Hult." (Mamita)

3/30 [1917]   Attend the "Olympic Exhibition". Reminds me of the exhibition five years ago, when I too was on the floor. The boys do splendidly. -- Banquet for the "Olympics" – *{He had taken Anna (Hagney) who had introduced him to Gertrude Jacobson on this occasion.}*

4/2   President Wilson reads his war-message to congress this evening. What will be the results?

4/4   War?! War?? – Beginning the writing of my Thesis for Apologetics. The question I have chosen I find so extensive and having such an abundance of material available for its treatment that it will be hard to make the proper selection.

"Mohammedanism." – One of the strongest foes the Chr. Church has to overcome today.

4/6   The threatening war cloud has broken upon our heads. WAR! The hour of our sinful nations 's reckoning has come. "War · Declared!"

4/7   War talk here, there, and everywhere! – Call at home of Dr. Foss. He believes that this war will usher in a new era of missions. God grant it!

4/10-11 Today my thesis is to be finished and corrected. Read the last page of it about 5:00 o'clock. I feel so thankful that this burden is now rolled off.

Seems good to resume the regular class work again, after having spent two weeks of interesting study in the room. Those who have been fortunate enough to have been away from the city a few days

{Easter vacation} return but hope that the variation of regular class-work will prove restful. I cannot hope to rest now till the last examination has been taken.

4/13   Chapel exercises – A real opportunity. – IT IS DONE! – *{He had asked Gertrude to go with him to the Lyceum lecture that evening - their first date.}*

4/16   An officer from the island speaks to us at the gym. War has now come to our doors! – The College Band has decided to enlist.

4/17   Many of the boys are down at the Armory, and some enlist. Magney has a hard time to come to a decision.

A letter from Leslie – "War!" -- It has now crossed over the threshold of my own peaceful home. Help us to do our duty before Thee and the Flag.

4/18   War! War! War! Chapel. Dr. Bartholomew announces the decision of the faculty that any student who enlists now will be given credit for the work of the rest of the term. Talk of organizing a "Company" from Augustana Mass meeting at the Gym. Disussions – but it is too late to discuss now. It is here and now!

G– J– is a visitor at our Volunteer Band meeting. – Teach us to do Thy will, oh God.

4/27   G– has now become a Student Volunteer. Thank God! There are some who hear the call and respond. God bless this decision, this new member of our band at Augustana.

4/30   Sunrise prayer meeting on Zion Hill with only three present. G– reads Romans 10 and asks that her parents be remembered in our prayers. – That very much worn Testament looks so good to me. What more can I wish for! Teach me, oh God, to do Thy will.

Mamita

A few minutes for prayer at Benson's, asking God's guidance and blessing upon the deliberations of our Board of Missions on the morrow.

5/2   A beautiful day! Sunshine after many days of cloudy weather. Final exam in Greek. I am informed by two members of the Board of Missions of the action taken yesterday. "A conditional call to Africa, pending action of the Synod."

[…]

5/13   A most glorious spring morning! G– consents to a walk out toward Rock River before going to church. – The senior class of the seminary has charge of the services at the Salem Church, Moline. At Salem, with G–.

5/16   Volunteer Band picnic at Watch Tower in the afternoon. What a relief to get out in the country again. Everything is so fresh and green – supper. – The return through the woods and over the country road with G–. We return to "Zion Hill" weary in body but refreshed in mind.

I thank thee, oh Lord for this "good gift" which thou has let come to me in these latter days. – Thy will be done.

5/18   15 years ago today I stood before the altar at Bethany and confessed before the congregation my faith. I promised my God faithfulness. – Oh, God, forgive my sins of commission and of omission. Lord, increase my faith and help me ever to live a life dedicated to the service of thee and my fellow men. Amen!

5/25 Last regular chapel exercises for the year. A feeling of sadness steals over me. – Class meeting – sign the formal application for ordination, etc., etc. – Receive an encouraging letter from Dr. Kumm. – Gertrude has taken her last "exam" for the year so we are off for a tramp in the country. – "Watch Tower" and back again before supper. I needn't say that the walk in God's out-of-doors was thoroughly enjoyed.

Mamita

{This was the first entry with the name Gertrude written out}

5/28 Seminary commencement.

5/29 Gertrude has decided to stay over the Synod to help Mrs. Rydholm prepare the Ladies Dormitory for guests.

Gunderson leaves for Chicago. I am very thankful for the opportunity of spending these two days with him. – Thy will be done! – Take a few hours of much-needed rest. – Go for a long walk in the evening with Gertrude. "Long View".

5/30 Spend the evening with Anna, Herbert, and Gertrude. – Sad news on the way home! – A snare for Gertrude. She must be helped to avoid it. – "I will not." Thank God.

{This was probably the expectancy of her parents that she should join the Eastern Star, a lodge which was considered anti-Christian. Her refusal created a rift between her parents and her for some time.}

A very restless night. Much prayer for G– [Gertrude]. It almost seemed as though someone was about to rob this "good gift" from me. Help her, oh God, to realize the great danger she is in. Give her the needed strength to abide by the dictates of her conscience. – Amen! – A victory has been won, thank God!

Quoted from a typoscript: Two Years in the Life of Ralph Hult. Excerpts from diaries, 1917 and 1919. Edited by Adeline Hult. 1991. Adeline, who was married to Mamita's son John, added several editorial remarks, which are marked {italics}.

SUDAN UNITED MISSION AND DR. KARL KUMM (1902)

The Sudan United Mission (S.U.M) was established in 1902 by Karl Kumm and his first wife, Lucy Guiness. Its primary objective was to evangelize the peoples of Adamawa and the Upper Benue region. Adamawa, a former German colonial territory, was later divided by the Nigerian-Cameroon border, while the Upper Benue encompasses parts of present-day Benue, Taraba, Plateau, and other northwestern states of Nigeria, as well as northern Cameroon.

Despite the initial statement of aims mentioning "the peoples" of the area, the mission's strategy focused on converting Animists rather than Muslims. A promotional pamphlet from the early days explicitly targeted the "host of heathen nations," emphasizing the need to introduce Christianity before these peoples embraced Islam.

In 1909, the Sudan United Mission launched the "Forward Movement" with the objective of evangelizing native tribes in the Sudan not yet influenced by Islam. The movement sought public support and recruits to establish 50 stations manned by at least 150 missionaries along the border between Islam and Paganism, along the sixth to eighth degrees latitude from the Niger to the Nile.

However, Kumm's mission encountered political resistance, largely emanating from Europe. This resistance compelled him to devise new strategies for his ventures within the Sudan belt, leading him to undertake extensive expeditions on the Niger and the Nile.

Karl Kumm was known for being an intrepid adventurer and a bold missionary explorer, drawn to the unknown and willing to face difficulties and obstacles. His writings consistently exuded optimism about the success of the mission.

The outbreak of World War I shook Western beliefs in the superiority of Western culture, impacting Kumm's career. He was forced to move to the United States of America, maintaining a vital relationship with the S.U.M as the General Secretary of the American branch. However, this relationship was no longer as dominant as it had been before the war, leading to a wavering of Kumm's optimism.

He is the author of: The Sudan. A short compendium of facts and figures about the land of darkness. (London 1907); From Hausaland to Egypt, through the Sudan (London 1910); Khont-Hon-Nofer: the lands of Ethiopia (London 1910).

> *Source: German Wikipedia article, "Karl Kumm". Jan H. Boer, The Last of the Livingstones: H. Karl W. Kumm's Missiological Conception of Civilization (Faculty of Theology, Free Reformed University of Amsterdam, 1973. Revised 2014).*

RALPH HULT ABOUT KARL KUMM (1917)

[In Ralph Hult's diary entries, we witness a profound admiration for Karl Kumm's personality, their encounters leaving a lasting impression on him. However, amid this admiration Ralph grapples with conflicting opinions about Kumm from others and Kumm's advice to the Mission Board to send Ralph out as an unmarried man, contrary to the counsel of other experienced missionaries. These entries offer a glimpse into Ralph's internal struggle as he contemplates his future mission work in Africa and the potential separation from Gertrude, causing uncertainty and emotional tension.]

1/27 [1917] Write Dr. Kumm, bidding him welcome to our Seminary to speak to us of his travels in the Sudan. -- May Thy Kingdom come, even to darkest Africa.

1/31 Volunteer Board meets and agrees to lay the matter of the proposed Mission work of our synod in Africa before God in prayer, asking that His will may be done. Coming home to the room, I find a letter from Dr. Kumm in which he accepts the invitation from our school to speak here on Africa."

51

Mamita

[...]

3/2 (7 A.M.) At the C.B. & A station to meet Dr. Kumm. Bring him to school and he speaks at the Chapel Exercises. – Speaks again before the Concordia Society. – My heart is too full to make any comments! Dr. Kumm has kindled a fire in our hearts for Africa. From 7 to 9 o'clock, he meets with the Committee appointed by the Mission Board to investigate the possibility of taking up work in Africa. John Benson and I are present at this meeting. A good meeting.

3/3 May God bless Dr. Kumm's visit at our school, that something definite may result from it.

3/8 Mission study Class on "The Dark continent" – Find that Dr. Kumm's visit has thrown a new light on many of the interesting facts we find in our textbook. – The "Chicago Tribune" for today has an announcement that 11 missionaries are today sailing for Africa to fill stations vacated by the Germans. – Would that I were ready to go."

[...]

6/30 Letter from Dr. Kumm. His reply to our questions as to what is meant by an 'affiliation with the Sudan United Mission' is hardly satisfactory.

7/3 How shall I reply to Dr. Kumm's letter? I shall be very frank with him so as to make the position of our Synod clear from the start. – Help me, oh God, in this thing.

[...]

1919

1/1 The dying moments of the year of grace 1918 and the first few moments of the new year are spent in the living room of Dr. Kumm's home at Summit, N.J., on our knees in prayer to God. – Bless, oh Lord, my Gertrude, whom Thou hast given me, with Thy choicest blessings. Keep her, oh Thou, who hast conquered sin and the consequences of sin. Keep me. Help us to live a victorious life, to be more than conquerors through Him. – Thou knowest how we long for the day, "vår stora dag", when we shall be joined in hand as well as in heart. If that will be one of the days of this year, we would seek Thy blessing. Prepare us for that great event in our life. – Oh, Father, Thou knowest how much we desire to get to go out into the "field" together and to take up the work at the same time. Help us to know Thy will for us in this matter. Teach, instruct, and counsel us, we pray. Thy will be done.

Spend all of New Year's Day at the Kumm's home with his large maps of Africa spread out before us on the floor. -- Where will the future Augustana Mission be? May God direct us to the place where he can use us best. -- Another of the topics of our conversation is "Gertrude" my Gertrude. (Mrs. Kumm's name is Gertrude). -- Dr. K. does not favor the idea of her going with me to Africa for a few years. God only knows what such a long wait means for me, and still may His will, not mine, be done.

1/21 At Princeton University. The meeting of the S.U.M. Council is held in the YMCA building of the University. Here I meet Miss Venstraa, who has been appointed as an S.U.M. missionary from the Dutch Reformed Church in America. She reminds me so very much of Gertrude that I enjoy the pleasant conversation with her as we wait to be introduced to the council. But it becomes a long wait. It appears that these gentlemen have forgotten that they have called us to come a long distance to attend this meeting. At last, we are ushered into the council room -- we expect to find a considerable group of men (according to the long list of names given in S.U.H. literature and stationery) -- but to our amazement, there are only three besides Dr. Kumm. -- After this disappointment (for me it was a disappointment), we spent a few pleasant minutes with these men. After a few minutes of prayer, we went to a College Inn for our supper. Then off to catch the train for New York -- How should I justify my time spent in coming all the way from Hartford for those few minutes with the council (in this case represented by these four gentlemen). Although invited by Dr. Kumm and advised to go by Dr. Kumm, I did not feel that it had been worthwhile.

3/2 For the past weeks and months, there has been a question that has occupied Gertrude's and my mind much. We do so wish to know God's will as to our going out together to Africa or not this year if the way should open up. – Should we decide here and now to act on Dr. K's advice, or should we push the matter? After much prayer and thought, we have decided to lay the matter before Father and Mother Jacobson to see how they would feel about Gertrude going to Africa with me at this time. In the meantime, we have prayed that the Spirit of God might direct the answer of Father and Mother. If they should, in any way, discourage it, we would take that as God's will for us, and Gertrude would then plan to take up some form of special preparation after completing her college studies in May. If, on the other hand, they should give us their assent, we would proceed to lay the matter before the members of the Board to see if they would favor such an arrangement and proceed to make preparations for Gertrude's going with me to Africa when I go out. – I have felt that under the circumstances Gertrude should lay this matter before her parents, and this she has already attempted to do. At her last visit home, the question was at last opened. – Now I feel it my duty to try to explain the whole situation to Father and Mother. This I have done today in a long letter addressed to them. – May God's will be done.

3/7 A message from Gertrude – "Father and Mother satisfied and happy." – Can it be true that they are satisfied to have their daughter enter into a work that will separate them from their daughter so much sooner than they had expected? In a short while, I send a reply to Gertrude – "What God hath wrought" – but doesn't it seem too good to be true, and yet it is in accord with the advice based on the experience of so many in whose judgment I have full confidence, and especially when it comes from the experience of

Mamita

missionaries. But why should our friend Dr. K. insist so persistently that Gertrude wait for a time? – Why?

[...]

3/14-16 Student Volunteer conference at Bloomington, Ill. of which Gertrude is the secretary and in the preparation of which she has spent so much time and effort. -- May He sustain my Gertrude so that the physical and mental strain of the past weeks and months may not prove too much for her. I have felt anxious about her. She has been endowed with an exceptionally strong body, and an unusual amount of energy, but there is a limit. – Dr. Kumm is to be one of the speakers at this conference. Gertrude will thus have an opportunity of meeting him for the first time. Having written to several of the Board members as well as to Dr. Kumm, we are now praying that this may prove to be a further confirmation of the good news from Father and Mother J. only a few days ago. If only Dr. K. meets Gertrude and has a good talk with her, will he not be ready to change his judgment and advice when he is to meet with our Board of Missions in a few days? Ske din vilja, o Gud!

3/18 Board meeting at Rock Island with Dr. Kumm present. Thy will be done! Give us grace to accept it, as it is made known to us.

3/21 Letter from Gertrude. Ske din vilja, o Gud! It seems that I shall have to go to Africa without Gertrude this first time. A walk by myself. A sense of peace comes over me that I have not experienced for a long time. Now it seems clear to us beyond any doubt, what God would have us do. We shall try to be satisfied. He doeth all things well.

3/23 Mother's Birthday. Mother. How I should like to talk over with her some of the problems that are facing me just now. A mother always understands her boy. God bless and keep my dear Mother.

3/25 Supper at (friend's) house. A very pleasant evening, **but some remark made as to the estimate of Dr. K. among missionaries**

in Egypt makes me feel very unhappy. Dr. K. is a very close friend of mine. His influence in my life thus far has been very large. It grieves me to hear what I have this evening. **I do want to believe that it is the result of his being misunderstood.**

3/28 Message from Dr. Kumm inviting me to spend the weekend at his home. He has just returned from the West. It will, therefore, be most pleasant to meet him at this time to receive greetings from home. Then, too, **I shall want to know definitely his grounds for advising my Board as he has with regard to Gertrude's going with me when most every missionary advises me to go out married rather than unmarried.**

> *Quoted from a typoscript: Two Years in the Life of Ralph Hult. Excerpts from diaries, 1917 and 1919. Edited by Adeline Hult. 1991.*

RALPH HULT ASKING FOR GERTRUDE JACOBSON'S HAND (9/20/1917)

> *But before he left, Ralph wanted our engagement to be official. He had already written to my parents, seeking their permission to marry me, and they had given their consent.*
> *(Mamita)*

To Mr. and Mrs. Jacobson, Geneseo, Illinois

Kind Friends,

Although late, I wish to thank you most heartily for the very pleasant five days spent at your home now a month ago. I assure you, those days were thoroughly enjoyed from the first to the last, and I appreciate more than I can tell all that you did to make me feel at home at Maplehurst. I feel at home there. For one grown up on a farm, it is always a most enjoyable experience to get away from the noise and bustle of the city to the peace and quiet of the country. "Come again!"... I shall only be too glad to come again, whenever the opportunity affords itself.

I love Maplehurst. Why? Because I love Gertrude and Maplehurst is her "Home, Sweet Home." There live her father and mother, her brothers and sisters. Around it center all the associations of the days of her childhood and youth. To her, there is no place in all the wide world like Maplehurst, her home. Little wonder then that I shall always number those days spent there among the "most pleasant of my life."

Yes, I love Gertrude... I had been at school only a few days last September when I first saw Gertrude. Her open and honest face, her unassuming manners at once attracted my attention. Although we first met after Christmas, long before that time, I realized that what at first was merely an attraction for Gertrude's personality soon had grown into admiration... My work during the summer months of the past few years has brought me into hundreds, not to say thousands, of homes in different states of our Union from the Atlantic to the Pacific, from Canada to old Mexico, and in these homes I have met with a great number of people, but among them all, I have never yet found a young woman who so nearly corresponds to my ideal of a life companion, a wife... To make real sure that my thoughts of Gertrude were not only for the time and therefore would soon pass away, I waited several months before showing her any attention, but all this time I saw her daily around the school and therefore had a good opportunity to study her and satisfy myself as to whether or not my first impressions of her were correct. All this time, too, I was praying to God to give me the needed wisdom to judge correctly in this matter because I have always considered the choice of a companion for life to be one of the most important, if not the most important, step we ever take in this life, a step which should hardly be made without invoking divine guidance. It was not before toward the end of the school year that I first met Gertrude to speak to her. On the evening of the 13th of April, we were together for the first time when I invited her to attend a lecture of the Augustana Lyceum Course with me. I had had many doubts as to whether or not I would be doing the right thing in seeking to form a closer acquaintance with Gertrude, but those doubts were all done away with that first evening we were together. My admiration was fast becoming love. Not many weeks later, I began to realize that Gertrude loves me, and I assure you, I know not how to thank God enough for the experience of that love and sympathy because I regard her love as a gift from Him. This feeling for each other has constantly grown in intensity, and we have now reached a point where we firmly believe that God has meant our lives to be spent together and that we, therefore, should hesitate no longer to unburden our hearts to our parents and by doing that to ask of them to set their seal of approval on what has thus come into our life during the past year. I am very glad to tell you that my mother has already given her most hearty approval. She was at Rock Island last June to be present at my ordination, and at that time, she met Gertrude. And now, Father and Mother Jacobson, may we ask of you to grant your approval?

I realize that I am asking of you very, very much when I thus ask of you the hand of your daughter. She represents much sacrifice on the part of her parents, who have done so much for her. You have spared nothing to give her the very best of education, and I believe I can realize just a little of what that means. It was my good father's one great ambition, while he lived, to give us a fair chance to get an education, and my good mother has worked so hard and sacrificed so much during all these years, and especially since Father was taken from us, to help us along. I know that I never shall be able to repay my good parents for all their toil and sacrifice for me, and I have had Gertrude tell me that she realizes that the same is true in her case. The most we can do is to try in every way to show to our parents our appreciation of what they have done and are doing for us, and then if God should see fit to entrust to us the rearing of children to perpetuate the memory of our parents by doing the same for our children. Yes, I do realize that I am asking much, very much, when I ask you to give the hand of your daughter.

"Who are you?" I hear you say. "We would like to know you better before we, by the bestowal of the hand of our daughter, could recognize you as a son." Perhaps a few facts from my life would best answer that question.

I was born in Kearney, Nebraska, on July 9, 1888. At that time, my father was in the hardware business but sold out three or four years later and bought a farm near Axtell, Nebraska, where we lived until 1907. I was the oldest of the children, and my father was farming quite heavily, so I had to begin working in the fields very early.

My attendance at school was not very regular. Some years I could attend only three or four months during the winter, but I still passed my eighth-grade examinations in the county when I was fifteen years old. The year before, I had finished my catechetical instruction and was thus received into communicant membership of the church. Now (1903), I wished so much to continue my studies, but it seemed impossible for my parents to spare me from the work on the farm at this time, until my younger brothers had grown up. I had to wait three years more before beginning my High School work. In the fall of 1906, I started Luther Academy at Wahoo, Nebraska. The following fall, my parents rented the farm and moved to Wahoo for the purpose of giving us children the best possible opportunity to go to school. We had been there only a few weeks when my father died as a result of an accident. As the oldest of eight children, I had to step in and try to take my father's place in the family until we could get settled in our new home. This put me back a year in my school work, but in May 1910, I graduated from Luther Academy. The following September, I enrolled at Augustana College of Rock Island and graduated from there three years later (1913). The following year was spent as a traveling missionary with the Utah Gospel Mission, doing work in Utah and Arizona. In September 1914, I entered the Chicago English Lutheran Seminary at Maywood, Illinois. Here I spent two years. A year ago this month, I came back to Rock Island to finish my theological studies at the Augustana Seminary. On the 28th of last May, I graduated from the Seminary and was thereby recommended to the Augustana Synod for ordination. Sunday, June 17th, I was ordained to the office of the ministry in the Lutheran Church, and the following day, I was commissioned by the President of the Synod as a missionary to Sudan, Africa, and am now in the service of the Augustana Board of Missions. Next Wednesday (Sept. 26th), this Board meets at Rock Island to perfect the plans for beginning this work in Africa. I am invited to be present at this meeting. From there, I will very likely be sent to some school in the East to take up further studies as a special preparation for the special work ahead of me.

Another question, "Can we feel reasonably sure that you could give Gertrude a good home, and this especially since you propose to take her with you to Africa someday?" Since July 1st, I am drawing a regular salary at the rate of 1,000 dollars a year and traveling expenses to and from the field. The Board provides the missionaries with homes and the needed buildings for the work. The salary of the married missionary is considerably higher than that of the unmarried, and for the education of the missionaries' children, a special allowance is given for each child. The missionaries are granted frequent furloughs of about a year at a time.

I have an insurance policy of 1,000 dollars and am also a member of the Pension and Aid Fund of the Augustana Synod. Then, too, there is my part in our estate, which consists of 200 acres of Nebraska farm land with improvements and two properties here in

Mamita

Wahoo. If God grants health and strength and with a right use of the resources available, I feel confident that Gertrude shall lack nothing for her comfort and welfare.

"When would you expect Gertrude to join you in Africa?" This would depend on circumstances which can hardly be foreseen now, but it would seem to be best for her to finish her two years in college and then, if possible, to take a year of special medical training. Thus she could be at home three years more. Since it devolves upon me to begin our work in Africa, the most that I could do during my first visit there would be to locate the field and study conditions, and then in a year or two, come back to make a report and to return to Africa later with a whole company of missionaries. When I would thus be ready to return a second time, I would hope that Gertrude could come with me.

I fear that this letter is becoming altogether too lengthy, so I must bring it to a close. I hope you will pardon my entrusting such an important message to a letter, but it seemed my only choice at present. May I look for an answer to this letter addressed to me at Rock Island, General Delivery, if possible, not later than Monday or Tuesday. If the Board should decide to send me first, I would be leaving Thursday or Friday and probably not be back before next summer. But before leaving, I should so much like to place a ring on Gertrude's hand, and nowhere would I rather do that than at Maplehurst in the presence of her parents.

Awaiting a favorable reply, I remain most respectfully and sincerely,

Ralph D. Hult

> *Typoscript found with the original letter and envelope in the family archives entitled: "Copy of letter written to Grandpapa and Grandma Jacobson asking for Gertrude Jacobson's hand in marriage—written in Wahoo, Nebraska, on Sept. 20, 1917."*

Fräulein A. Gertrud Beer

After Father's death.

After Father's death, our mother was left alone as a young woman of 35 with five children between the ages of two and twelve. None of us children fully understood what this death meant for us and that a whole new chapter of our lives had begun. But we three daughters felt how much our mother suffered and how the pain almost overwhelmed her. We tried to stick close to her. As an outward sign of this attempt, we decided not to call our mother "Mama" anymore because it seemed too childish. After much discussion, we agreed on "Muttel," and she remained our dear Muttel until her death 31 long years after Father's passing.

Those were sad Advent days! No pine branches! No candles! No anticipation of Christmas! That's why the joy that a dear friend of our father brought us on Christmas Eve made an unforgettable impression: Suddenly, the doorbell rang loudly and persistently at the front door. We all rush there at once and open it with great curiosity. Who could be coming now? - Nobody is there. But in front of us is a small, beautifully decorated Christmas tree, whose shining candles glow at us. - The greater the darkness, the brighter the light. So, we also had our Christmas joy!

No matter how heavy the blow may be, life goes on, and looking back, one must admit that this merciless continuation is a great mercy for our human life. - Soon, everything continued as usual for us too. We three school-aged girls trotted off to school every morning after the Christmas holidays. We had moved to Kronprinzstraße at Easter 1900. Since the elementary school my sisters had attended until then was too far away, they went to the newly opened "Higher School for Girls" in Schletterstraße, and I was also enrolled there. It was the first ten-class girls' school for Leipzig, to which Hugo Gaudig, previously a professor at the Francke Foundations in Halle an der Saale, was appointed director.

My School Days

I was almost seven years old at the time. Thanks to my two older sisters, I could already read, write, and do arithmetic. My memory of my early school days is of almost unbearable boredom, which I tried to escape by getting up to all sorts of mischievous pranks.

I still remember my first day of school very clearly, or rather the way home from school. I probably walked to school with my sisters early in the morning, but I don't remember for sure. Our maid was supposed to pick me up at noon because my sisters had classes that went on later. But no one was there to pick me up. So, I decided to make my way home alone. It was the most straightforward school route imaginable in a big city. From our house at the corner of Kronprinz- and Elisenstraße, it led straight to the school at the intersection of Elisen- and Schletterstraße. We three sisters had been talking for weeks about how many streets we had to cross, and we soon knew them by heart, making bets on who could recite them the fastest (Kronprinz-, Moltke-, Arndt-, Schenkendorf-, Körner-, Sophien-, Sidonien-, Hohe and Schletterstraße), forwards, backward, and so on. So, I stopped at every street corner and spelled out the white, highly ornate letters on the blue signs. It must have been a comical sight, this tiny little girl with her satchel on her back, spelling out every oh-so-tall street sign. But I arrived home, albeit quite late, feeling very proud, and was greeted with a sigh of relief because the maid had tried to pick me up at school and had returned without me.

I started school on Easter 1900. Three years later, we had to start living without our loving father and caring head of the household. While we certainly did not experience any hardship - our mother received a widow's pension and had a small income from the family property in Moschelesstraße - some restrictions were necessary. Above all, the large six-room corner apartment was too expensive and no longer necessary. So, we soon moved to a smaller apartment on the same floor. But my mother could only endure these cold, sunless rooms, whose windows all faced north except for the kitchen, for two and a half years. Already at Easter 1906, we moved a few streets further south to Brandvorwerkstraße 85. It was a brand new house, almost the southernmost in the city, and it was wonderful there! About 500 meters of open land separated us from the suburb of Connewitz to the south. We had a small garden behind the house and a balcony at the front and back. Opposite, in the west, a lush wheat field swayed in the summer breeze, immediately followed by the forest of the Pleißenaue.

If this house could speak, I wouldn't have to write down many things now. I experienced so much there: the death of my grandmother in 1909, which cast a shadow over the dance class, the final exams after ten years of school in 1910, the entrance exam to the teacher training college, and three years later, the final state exam, the second exam two years later, the wedding of my sister Hertha in the summer of 1913, the outbreak of World War I in 1914, the death of my brother Rudolf as a volunteer soldier in May 1915, the wedding of my sister Marie in 1920, my engagement in 1921, my wedding in 1922.

But first, I was still a 14-year-old girl. Another change coincided with the event of our move. As a second higher school for girls was needed in Leipzig, a modern school building was constructed in the north of the city. Gaudig moved there as director with his entire staff and many of the students. My sister Hertha and I also moved with them, as the new building housed the first municipal teacher training college we wanted to attend. Mariechen had already fulfilled her eight-year compulsory schooling. As she did not enjoy learning as much as we did but was very practical and skillful, she stayed home with Mother to help with household chores and let us dismiss the maid, who was very expensive under our current circumstances.

Our new school route was four kilometers long, which took us an hour to cover. So, day after day, we set out at seven in the morning and returned at two o'clock, and later in the training college, classes sometimes began at seven or lasted until two. But classes were never in the afternoon. We only rarely used the tram, as it was too expensive, but the long school journey was never a burden to me. There was always something to learn, see, and chat about. We were not the only ones who walked. Gaudig, who lived near the Schletterstraße, remained there until his death. Long after my school days, he once told me that he used to look out for me every day at a particular spot and adjust his pace accordingly. He never again experienced such "Kantian punctuality." - When we later got a bicycle, which we had to share, the long school journey no longer took up quite as much time. - But one great advantage of moving to the new school was that my entire education happened in the same learning environment, which is seldom the case.

Since our earliest childhood, we all went to our grandparents' house on Sunday afternoons at Moschelesstraße. They owned the large, three-story corner house, and the fact that our Muttel later received a regular supplement to the widow's pension from this property made her life significantly easier.

I often found it boring at my grandmother's house; incidentally, she was my grandfather's second wife, and I never had an inner connection to her. So, I often went to the garden and played ball with my little sister. The garden faced the street, and on the other side of the road, there lived a teacher whose oldest son watched me and later often came down to us. He was my first admirer.

On our way to the grandfather, we would cross the Scheibenholz and Albert Park. An ice rink was set up on a frozen pond in winter. This is where we learned to ice skate. Our parents took us there, put on our ice skates, and then waved for a student to come and hold each child. Meanwhile, our parents gracefully glided over the ice surface. To the credit of the neighbor's boy, the teacher's son, I did not remain stuck at the beginner level of ice skating but soon - safely guided - flew over the mirror-smooth ice surface in a waltz rhythm.

Mutti

Alexander Eisenschmidt

Around the year 1904, we made the acquaintance of
Alexander Eisenschmidt. It was, strictly speaking, a
chance encounter during a journey. We were traveling
with Mother to a summer resort, a village near Moor-
bad Schmiedeberg by the Elbe River. The train was
overcrowded, and we stood tightly squeezed between
the benches. Suddenly, two large hands reached out
for our three or four-year-old Irmgard, and a kind
voice with a slightly unfamiliar German accent asked,
"May I hold the little one on my lap?" He placed her
on his knee and chatted so skillfully with her that she
immediately became trusting and stayed with him for
the entire journey. We had the same destination. He
was a student at the Leipzig Missionary Seminary and
was traveling to Schmiedeberg for treatment because
he suffered from severe rheumatism. He was from
Estonia and couldn't go home during the holidays, so
he was delighted when Mother invited him to visit us
at our summer retreat. By the end of the following
weeks, the chance encounter had turned into a close
family friendship.

As a young person, Eisenschmidt felt lonely among
the spa guests, so he came to visit us almost daily, and
soon he became indispensable to us. He took us on
long walks in the forest, and when my sister Irmgard
no longer wanted to walk, he patiently carried her in
his arms. He went mushroom picking with us, knew

where to find the most beautiful blackberry bushes, and was tireless in collecting those flavorful fruits. I don't remember the specifics of his relationship with each of us. He held high regard for Muttel and sought to support her in any way he could, especially in raising our brother Rudi, whose fatherless upbringing was all too apparent. Hertha, who was already fourteen, probably saw him as a young man. But Mariechen and I clearly had a playful teasing relationship with him. Wherever possible, we would make fun of him. At first, we came up with a nickname, "Eisi." -- Once, when he politely bid farewell to Muttel, who was lying in the hammock in the garden and stumbled over the mushrooms we had spread out to dry, the two of us couldn't help but burst into laughter.

It is only natural that this friendship continued in Leipzig. We were so accustomed to Eisi's visits that they didn't disturb our activities. Perhaps I was the least affected, once prompting him to remark, "I can come whenever I want. Gertrud is always studying." But that was certainly an exaggeration. I vividly remember, for example, heated competitions playing drum ball right in front of the house or pleasant walks in the woods where we always had to sing "Im schönsten Wiesengrunde" in three-part harmony. He often picked us up in winter for ice skating on the Pleiße.

Mutti

Teacher Training College (1910-1912)

When my training at the teacher training college began at Easter 1910, it was by no means a given for a middle-class girl to pursue a profession. At that time, working-class children entered apprenticeships after eight years of school and became workers. The "middle class" attended some advanced school, usually private, or completed a ninth and tenth year of school, while the daughters of the "upper ten thousand" were sent to boarding school for a year, often abroad. They learned foreign languages there and received the so-called "finishing touch." Upon their return, they remained in their parents' homes, engaged in handicrafts, pursued music and dance, and waited for a husband.

Many of my classmates expected this path, looked forward to it, and looked down upon me with obvious pity. However, this pity did not last long. When I became financially independent in 1913, when the hardships of war set in, when young men died by the hundreds, things looked very different.

As for me, I did not consider myself worthy of pity. I was delighted to have the opportunity to become a teacher. I consciously and joyfully chose this profession and have never regretted it. Throughout my life, I have thoroughly enjoyed teaching. Even in 1959, at the age of 66, I resumed teaching. I visited my children in Cameroon and was asked to teach German to beginner classes at the secondary school. This teaching captivated me so much that I forgot everything around me, even the fact that these were African boys learning the German language.

The director of the teacher training college was Hugo Gaudig. He was a gifted educator. Breaking with many traditions, he gave his school an entirely new character, focusing on the individual's education. The first condition for independent development is freedom. The form of instruction was free discussion. In the era of rote learning, this was so revolutionary that many educators traveled from afar to observe Gaudig and learn about his new teaching method. Twice I had the privilege of enjoying his pedagogical instruction for a year, and even today, I regard this towering intellect with awe. However, he also appointed only the best teachers to his staff. Thanks to the excellent French instruction I received from the same teacher for ten years, I was able to teach the German language to my Cameroonian students, most of whom had different African mother tongues, nearly 50 years after leaving the seminar.

Gaudig's generous and liberal approach was evident to anyone who entered our school building during a break. It was almost complete chaos. No one thought of proper behavior or orderly descent on the stairs. When a visitor pointed out the dangers of such unruliness, Gaudig laughed, "It's strange, but no accidents ever happen!"

After passing the final examination, I worked as a private tutor in Vogtland. The manor was near Plauen. Gaudig had chosen this position because he believed my energy made me suitable. He recognized this quality in me early on and derived many benefits for his school from it.

He borrowed many books from the university library and passed them on to the students for study. He was not overly concerned with returning the often valuable books as befits a genius. When the reminders had piled up too much, he would give me the entire stack of overdue notices, entrusting me with collecting and returning those books. I held this position for three years during my time at the college. The first place I searched was the enormous table in the middle of the study room in Gaudig's apartment, where books of all kinds piled up haphazardly and in large quantities. There, I spent many, many hours trying to find them. For the books that I couldn't find there, I had to rely on my fellow trainee teachers to track them down. And when a book couldn't be located, which happened quite often, I had to bear the librarian's reproach. However, there were moments when I was invited for coffee or dinner, which greatly rewarded my efforts.

Gaudig, or "Rex," as we called him, was very good to me. He would give me some of his published books and add a personal dedication as a token of appreciation. And when I passed the final examination at the graduation ceremony and asked him for an autograph, he wrote diagonally across the entire page in Greek letters, using a red pencil, "energeia," which means "energy."

That was the reason why he recommended me for Rittergut Liebau.

House Teacher (1913)

As a private tutor, my role as a house teacher would be to provide education and guidance to the young boy Philipp, whose mother was a widowed estate owner. It would be my responsibility to prepare him for his future academic endeavors, particularly his admission to the Realschule in Plauen. Despite his initial reluctance to study, as he believed he would eventually inherit the Liebau estate and saw no need for formal education, I was determined to instill a sense of curiosity and the importance of learning. The concerned mother had approached Gaudig and her brother-in-law, a pastor in Leipzig, seeking his assistance. So, unsuspecting and excited one Friday evening, I returned from a choir rehearsal at the Thomaskirche I regularly attended. On this particular occasion, as always, I met my long-time friend from the dance class, and we had, as often happened, argued about a problem in an Ibsen drama we had seen at the theater. He was over 30 centimeters taller than me and always walked on the roadway close to the curb, giving me the advantage of the height difference. As soon as I entered the front hallway, Muttel greeted me, saying, "Where have you been? Pastor H. has been waiting for you for an hour. He really wants to meet you." This did not fit my mood, so I answered probably too loudly, "Oh, so I'm supposed to take care of that unruly boy after all!" and threw my hat on the table. At that moment, the door opened. Pastor H. laughed and said, "Yes, indeed, you are supposed to, and I firmly believe you will handle him just fine!"

So, twice recommended, "little Beer" or "Beerlein" embarked on her journey to Rittergut Liebau in the Vogtland in April 1913. The train station was Jocketa. And what did she do? Instead of boarding the local train that stops at Jocketa, where she would be met with a carriage and horses, she foolishly boarded the express train, which did not stop at Jocketa!

Well, I still managed to reach my destination that evening. It was a wonderful time that followed. Fully embraced by the family, I took part in everything that the estate owners could afford at the time. I particularly enjoyed the rides through the charming Vogtland region in a carriage during the summer and in a sled during the winter. Outside of teaching hours, from 8:00 a.m. to 1:00 p.m., I had complete freedom and made the most of it. With my fellow trainee teacher who worked on a neighboring estate, I went on many hikes, mainly in the Vogtland, often venturing into the Erzgebirge on Saturdays and Sundays.

After three years of training at the seminar, nature appealed to me more than books. I gladly accompanied the lady of the manor on her evening walks through the fields, which often felt like explorations to me. I had never seen a blooming rapeseed field before, with its vibrant yellow later replaced by the delicate yellow-blue of flax. I also enjoyed helping with the morning strawberry harvest in the dewy hours before dawn. All the fruits that were not used in the household and most of the milk (there were 70 dairy cows), which was not used for cheese making, were transported daily to a nearby town, where a distribution office ensured their proper allocation. Every Saturday, the accounts had to be settled, and the money collected had to be brought back to Liebau. It took 20 minutes to reach the train station and another 10 minutes by train to reach the town. The path led through a small forest. I willingly and often volunteered to collect the money. On the way back, I sometimes had to climb up through the woods when dusk was falling. When asked if I was not afraid, I always responded, "If someone comes and wants the money, I will give it to them without hesitation!"

I thought I had settled into life. But first, there was something I needed to learn, namely the card game "Doppelkopf." Since my father had been a staunch opponent of card playing, I was unfamiliar with cards and had first to learn their ranking. I still remember reciting the order of cards aloud in bed at night. This way, I could participate in the evening games.

Initially, there was a disappointment in terms of teaching. In addition to Philipp, I was also assigned to instruct his older sister, who was 14 years old and was supposed to complete her "schooling." I had been looking forward to this opportunity and had made various plans, particularly for German literature and the French language. However, I found a young lady who showed little intellectual interest, had poor spelling skills, and was spoiled. As a result, I had to lower my expectations and focus solely on preparing her for finishing school, leaving everything else to the boarding school she would attend later.

On the other hand, Philipp did not disappoint me because I had no great expectations. I quickly gained his friendship by sitting in his cart, which a goat pulled, and letting him take me for rides. The condition for these outings was that he had to be in the schoolroom by seven o'clock in the morning, and I didn't have to search for him in all the stables. I made arithmetic more interesting for him by pretending to be estate owners and inspectors, and he always had to be cautious as his "inspector" might deceive him. With this approach, we managed to make progress, and he passed the entrance exam and entered the Realschule in Easter 1914. After another half year, his sister completed her schooling. My time as a house teacher came to an end in July 1914.

School Teacher (1914-1918)

In August 1913, my sister Hertha married an elementary school teacher. They had to fight for their happiness because, at that time, the separation between social classes was so strict that it was considered socially unacceptable for a professor's daughter to marry a mere elementary school teacher. During the following summer vacation, I spent time with my mother and youngest sister in the small town in Thuringia, where my brother-in-law was a teacher. During this vacation, the First World War broke out on August 1, which forced us to return to Leipzig immediately.

Since I had always planned to enter public service after my time as a house teacher, I immediately contacted the city's education authority and requested employment as an assistant teacher. However, Leipzig was not hiring new personnel due to the chaos of the first weeks of the war. But how could one sit idle at home when enthusiastic, hastily conscripted soldiers were marching through the streets singing, young men were volunteering for combat in large numbers, and the Red Cross called upon girls and women to enroll in first aid courses? I knew many young teachers had been conscripted for military service, leaving schools with a shortage of teaching staff. So, I decisively went to the elementary school nearest my apartment and offered my services to the principal. They gladly accepted my services after assuring them that I was willing to teach without pay. This was no small feat for me as a twenty-one-year-old, inexperienced teacher. Being small and delicate in stature – only 1.50 meters tall and weighing less than a hundred pounds – I knew from the beginning that I could only win the girls over, many of whom were 13 or 14 years old and much taller and sturdier than me, by treating them as equals, by being more of a friend than an authoritarian figure. I actually succeeded in establishing a good connection and creating an atmosphere conducive to effective teaching.

In 1915, just five months later, I finally got a position as a paid assistant teacher. I was appointed to an institution outside Leipzig that served as a transit camp for welfare children. The Heilerziehungsheim was connected to the mental hospital, and the children received medical care from the hospital's doctor. The children were observed, examined, and then directed to the appropriate educational institutions: psychiatric clinics, institutions for the mentally disabled, orphanages, or foster families.

To familiarize myself, I first studied the files of the children I would be caring for. Put it bluntly: a professor's sheltered daughter was exposed to the harsh realities of life. There were broken families, alcoholics who beat their wives and children, fathers who abused their daughters, free love, brothels, and so on. What did I know up until then? An orderly family life, socializing with like-minded people, and a passion for intellectual pursuits.

It required teaching under conditions we hadn't been trained for in the seminar, and I was unprepared for it. Externally, I had to get used to the fact that everything was designed to prevent the children from escaping. I would lock myself in the classroom with the class; even the windows could only be opened with a key. Discipline was a constant issue, and the actual teaching played a secondary role. All sorts of things happened! Someone would loudly complain about a missing shoe that couldn't be found, and another would pull out a bottle of beer from under their desk and start drinking. Another would rant about a poor grade and refuse to be silenced.

I still wonder how I dared to take such a class on an outing. But one day, I cheerfully set off early in the morning with ten girls. They were around 12 years old, excited for the day, and we sang hiking songs. Everything went well until our midday break. When it was time to resume our hike, four girls had mysteriously disappeared. In despair, I sought the nearest opportunity to make a phone call and contacted the institution's management. The reassuring voice of the director still echoes in my ear to this day: "Just come back with the remaining students, and the others won't get far in their institution uniforms. They will be brought back to us." And so it happened.

Meanwhile, the World War was raging outside and claimed many victims. On May 8, 1915, my only brother, a volunteer soldier, fell at the age of 19 in Ypres, Belgium.

In October 1915, I was appointed as a teacher to the 31st District School in Leipzig-Connewitz. The school's location, just a 20-minute walk from my home, was quite pleasant, although the principal, known as the strictest in Leipzig, was less so. However, I personally only received a scolding from him once, and I must admit he had a valid reason. Just before the autumn break, I learned that I was expected to begin my duties at the 31st District School on the first day of school. While it would have been appropriate for me to introduce myself earlier, I didn't consider it necessary and instead traveled to visit my sister in Thuringia, staying there until the last moment and arriving at my new school promptly on Monday morning. The principal received me somewhat despotically and with great suspicion, outlining my new responsibilities: "You will be teaching a sixth-grade and a second-grade class. Today, you have seven hours of teaching, from 8 a.m. to 1 p.m. and from 3 p.m. to 5 p.m. How do you plan to manage without any preparation?" I remained silent, for he was right. But I felt no fear, neither of him nor of the tasks ahead. Through my experiences at the Heilerziehungsheim, I had grown accustomed to many challenging situations and no longer shied away from them. The stern principal never discovered that I already had a ticket for the premiere of Peer Gynt, which lasted from 6 p.m. to 11 p.m. on that very Monday. As time went on, we developed a rather good rapport. The strict principal took a keen interest in modern pedagogy, particularly Gaudig's method of personality development. He read all of Gaudig's books and occasionally pulled me out of my class to discuss passages, asking, "Read this sentence! What is Gaudig trying to convey?" He even attended some of my lessons to observe Gaudig's concept of "self-directed student activity."

My teaching career progressed following the prescribed path. In September 1916, I successfully passed my second teaching examination. In April 1917, I became a provisional teacher, and finally, on January 1, 1919, I was appointed as a permanent teacher. Even the revolution in November 1918 initially had no impact on my professional journey.

MARRIAGE (1918-1922)

Mrs. Ralph Hult

Augustana (1918)

That year was fruitful for both of us in our respective schools. One of the highlights was the Missionary Conference of the Student Volunteer bands from colleges in Illinois, which took place at Knox College. About 20 students from Augustana, including myself, attended the conference. It was a valuable opportunity to meet missionaries and learn about their work.

It was decided that Ralph should continue his studies in Hartford so that he could graduate from the institution the following spring.

We also had the chance to attend the 1918 Synod meeting together, where we witnessed the ordination of many of our friends. Afterward, we visited Ralph's hometown of Wahoo, where I enjoyed getting to know his brothers and sisters. I had previously met his mother during Ralph's ordination in Rock Island, and spending time with her was a true delight. It was a joy for me to experience the fellowship of a Christian home, where daily devotions were held and where the center of everyone's activities revolved around the church and Jesus Christ.

During that summer, which took place during the war, many women were working in factories. My mother encouraged me to try for such a job, and I secured one in East Moline. I commuted to work every day using our Model T Ford.

Come September 1918, I returned to Augustana for my senior year of college. This time, I worked in the library to earn a portion of my expenses. The previous year, I had been involved in cleaning duties in the dormitory and washing and drying dishes in the dining hall. I thoroughly enjoyed my studies, my fellow students' company, and my professors' guidance. Dr. Andreen served as our president, and he was not only a friend to us students but also a source of inspiration through his life and teachings. I have vivid memories of his chapel talks—his enthusiasm and zeal. He reminded me greatly of my paternal grandfather, Peter Jacobson, who, after his conversion, seemed to possess many of the characteristics of Peter, the disciple of Jesus.

At college, there were numerous extracurricular activities available to students. I participated in the Glee Club, Mission Society, Bible classes, and basketball. I even had the privilege of participating in the annual students' oratorical contest. It was a fulfilling experience to delve into the subject I had chosen, "The Negro in America." Although I didn't win a placement in the contest, my oration was published in the

Lutheran Companion. Later, I received a copy of a South Carolina Negro newspaper that had reprinted my oration with favorable comments.

I was also asked to assist in planning the Student Volunteer Annual Missionary Convention for Illinois colleges. This conference held great significance for me. The president and vice-president elected the previous year were now serving in the armed forces. When the meeting took place, I was appointed as the chairman. We had the privilege of hosting several missionary speakers, including Dr. Kumm, the U.S. secretary of the Sudan United Mission. He had traveled extensively across Africa, including through the Sudan, and was an outstanding speaker.

Wedding (1919)

In our graduating class, there were four girls and around forty boys. Many of the boys had served in the armed forces and returned to school after the war to complete their education. My parents were present at my graduation, but Ralph couldn't attend as he was graduating from the School of Missions himself.

With the war now over, it seemed possible for Ralph to finally make his way to Africa. The Mission Board felt it was best for him to go alone to conduct survey work, although they agreed to our marriage before his departure. In early June, we decided to have our wedding on July 9th, 1919, which also happened to be Ralph's birthday.

We were married in our farm home, with the pastor of my church, Zion of Rock Island, officiating the ceremony. Ralph had to attend a board meeting earlier that day and arrived in the afternoon by train. The pastor and other guests were scheduled to arrive on the evening train. However, a heavy rain and thunderstorm kept my girlfriend in Rock Island, who was supposed to sing at the wedding. Fortunately, the pastor arrived safely. We had invited several of my aunts and uncles who lived nearby, but most of them could not attend due to the storm and muddy roads. However, as the rain and storm subsided, the evening turned beautiful. Although our wedding party was not large, it was a truly joyous occasion.

After the wedding, a charivari celebration was organized by the men and boys in the neighborhood. We were sitting at the table when the first shots were fired. A flurry of gunshots, a clattering of cans, and various other noises followed it. According to custom, such festivities were followed by treating the participants, and we were prepared for that.

The following day, we departed for Nebraska to visit Ralph's family in Axtell and Funk. During our journey, we also made a stop at Bethphage Mission. Reverend C.A. Lonnquist was serving as the Director of the Mission at that time. He had been Ralph's pastor at Bethany Church for many years and had provided invaluable pastoral counsel during Ralph's early adolescence. Ralph had a deep sense of his sinfulness, believing that he was such a terrible sinner that God couldn't possibly forgive him. However, his pastor helped him understand that once sins are confessed and forsaken, God forgives them, and the blood of Jesus covers them. The pastor's guidance and support had led Ralph to experience the joy of salvation, making him hold a special place in Ralph's heart.

After our visits, we returned to my home. Meanwhile, Ralph had been making efforts to arrange his journey to Africa. However, due to the disruptions caused by the war, shipping was still not back to normal, making it quite challenging. It was decided that Ralph should go to New York to explore possible arrangements. Fortunately, Ralph was successful in his endeavors and discovered that a freighter was scheduled to sail for West Africa in early November. He was accepted as a passenger on the ship.

There was little time left to prepare for his departure, so Ralph hurried back. I returned to my home while he bid farewell to his family in Wahoo. As Ralph's mother said her goodbyes, she uttered the words, "This is the happiest day of my life!" Ralph had been dedicated to the Lord even before he was born, and those words would be a source of comfort and blessing in the coming days.

Although my parents consented to my joining Ralph, they were not entirely pleased with the situation and struggled to understand it. Our remaining time together was limited, and there were only a few things I could do to help my husband prepare for the unknown. Getting his clothes ready was one of those tasks. In just a few days, he was all set. On the day of his departure, my father and mother accompanied us to the station in Moline. It was a difficult moment to bid him farewell. He waved from the steps of the train car until he was no longer visible in the distance.

Just before Ralph set sail for Africa on the SS Bereby, he made a final phone call to me from New York. It was a bittersweet moment as he embarked on his journey, leaving me behind in America when I longed to be by his side.

Before his departure, Ralph and I had made arrangements for me to spend the following months at the Immanuel Deaconess Institute in Omaha. During the initial weeks, I assisted in the Children's Home, which I found to be a fulfilling experience. It provided me with valuable knowledge on caring for babies and young children, skills that would prove useful later in our home.

After Christmas, I was assigned to work at the hospital, where I had the opportunity to learn and observe various medical procedures over the course of a few months. I vividly remember attending my first birth, witnessing my first surgery, and spending my first night on night duty, tending to a sick deaconess on her deathbed. These months of training were truly invaluable, both in my future role as a mother and as a missionary.

During the months of separation, visiting Ralph's home in Wahoo provided solace and support. Having a place to go that felt like home, with Mother Hult and his brothers and sisters, was comforting. These visits immensely helped me during our time apart.

WEDDING OF RALPH AND GERTRUDE HULT (7/9/1919)

7/9   At last our day has dawned. After all these long years of waiting for it, it has come at last.

Though knowest, O God, how we both have hungered for what our hearts now have found in each other. As our hearts have already been joined, we would now publicly acknowledge this love before our relatives and friends and be joined in matrimony.

Oh, God, in your mercy and grace, bless us. Amen!

Attend the meeting of the Board of Missions where I make known what is to take place at Maplehurst this evening. – There is every evidence that the members of the Board seem quite pleased by this announcement. I am instructed to try to rest up as much as possible, spending as much time as possible in the country and try to forget my books for a while. – Leave this meeting feeling beyond any doubt that the prayers and well-wishes of the Board follow us.

Mamita

Very busy shopping until [it was] time for the afternoon train for Colona. The last matter before leaving Moline is calling for Gertrude's bouquet {white Sweet Peas}. Gertrude meets me at Colona. How happy we are as we ride home!

We fear that the weather will not be what we might wish. Threatening clouds are beginning to appear in the west. – But we shall hope that all will be well. – As soon as we sit down for coffee a little after five, it is so dark that it is almost necessary to have a light. – Soon after, the storm breaks loose. Such a storm as it is! It is after six before it has passed over. Verne goes to Green River to meet Roy who comes out from Chicago on the six o'clock train.

It looks very improbable that the folks from Moline will be out in such roads as this. – Dr. Ekholm will no doubt wait for the train, so Father goes to meet him at Colona.

We are so pleased to see Brother Roy. – How I miss my folks. It does make me feel a bit sad to find that I shall not have a single representative of my own family present. Would it not have been possible for someone to have come? Of course, we hope to see Mother Hult and the brothers and sisters in a few days, but that cannot make up for their presence now.

But I do know that we are followed by Mother's prayers. We do have her blessing, as much as though she were present. She is very near to us this evening. The time for the ceremony has been set for eight o'clock but it will be later because Dr. Ekholm cannot possibly get here by that time if he is to come by train and then come over these roads from Colona.

The bride and groom have been ready for some time when we hear the announcement "The preacher has come!" – In a little while all is ready. – At the sound of the music (sister Mae at the piano) we enter the front room where the minister awaits us.

Mamita

The ritual used is that for "The Solemnization of Marriage" according to the "Church Book of the Evangelical Lutheran Augustana Synod in North America."

After our marriage has thus been solemnized, Dr. Ekholm directs a few words to us, using I Corinthians 13:13 as a text: "Now abideth faith, hope, love, these three; and the greatest of these is love."

After the ceremony Father and Mother, brothers and sister, relatives and friends give us their well-wishes and congratulations.

Now I am a member in the Jacobson family. From this hour my status is quite a different one in this home. God help me to be a dutiful son.

Then the wedding meal. Only half of the expected guests could come so we are all easily seated around a long table in the living room. Uncle Charlie and Auntie, Uncle Will and Auntie, Aunt Emma Stohl, Dr. Ekholm, Father and Mother, Mae, Roy, and Verne.

We do have such a pleasant time. Roy serves as the Toastmaster. He gives a few interesting anecdotes from the life in the Jacobson home. He chooses to call upon "the bride" and "the groom" to say something.

What shall I say? What can I say, but this, that I wish here in the presence of these relatives and friends to thank first of all Father and Mother Jacobson for the gift they have given me this day. Words fail me to express my appreciation of the privilege of being adopted into "the Jacobson tribe."

Dr. Ekholm responds by reading a message of congratulation from the Augustana Board of Missions. That message pleases us very much, since it indicates the approval of this body of this step even though Gertrude cannot go with me at this time to Africa.

Mamita

During the course of the meal, there was an interruption. We had scarcely been seated when all at once a volley of guns was heard apparently from all sides of the house. After the shots came a peculiar sound that almost sounded like the breaking of every window pane in the house. – When we thought that the ammunition was pretty well exhausted, we ventured forth to see who the uninvited visitors might be. Imagine our surprise when we found the neighbors for some miles around (perhaps thirty or forty in all), old and young ones. We were quite pleased to realize that they had come out in such roads to show their interest in us. After passing around the cigar box and offering those who did not smoke some ice cream, they quietly withdrew. We were none the worse for this bit of excitement except little Charlie and poor old "Shep," who were both dreadfully frightened.

The meal over, the evening was quietly spent in a social way. It seemed so homelike, just a sort of family gathering. Not until after midnight did the folks leave for home or retire.

Now, as we were alone, I could really see the bride. How well she looked in her veil. How proud we both felt of Mother and Father, making her daughter's wedding outfit. It had surely been a labor of love on her part. Who knows what thoughts have moved in the parents' hearts this evening as they have seen their daughter as a bride. God bless Father and Mother. How shall I ever repay them for the gift they have given me this day?

Our Prayer

Oh, God, in your mercy and grace, bless us and guide us, that Thy way may be known upon earth and Thy salvation among all the nations.

God bless our home.

Mamita

May we love Thee with all our heart and all our mind and soul. Without Thy constant presence and blessing the joys that we now are experiencing in each other's love will soon fade away. Oh, God, bless us and keep us even to the end through our Lord Jesus Christ. Amen!

We have come to the end of "var stora dag." And now Gertrude Leona is mine, and Ralph Daniel is hers.

May nothing ever come into our hearts and lives to mar the joys of this day. Sorrows and disappointments may, yes, surely will, come, but we have before God and our fellow men promised to love each other in adversity as well as prosperity.

> *Quoted from a typoscript: Two Years in the Life of Ralph Hult. Excerpts from diaries, 1917 and 1919. Edited by Adeline Hult. 1991.*

West Africa (1920-1921)

The summer quickly passed, and it was time for me to return home and prepare for my journey to Africa. When Ralph first arrived in Africa, he met the Guinter family, missionaries with the Sudan United Mission. They were planning to return to Africa after a furlough and had graciously agreed to travel with me to their station, where I would finally be reunited with Ralph.

Saying farewell to my family was not easy. My father and mother expressed their feelings, saying, "It seems you are going so far away." I distinctly remember the final moments at the Geneseo depot with my father before boarding the train to Chicago.

During my journey, I made a stopover at Niagara. It was a cold and gloomy day in early December when I first laid eyes on the magnificent Falls. That night, I found myself back on the train, heading towards New York City. At that time, no Women's Home was provided by the Women's Missionary Society, so I arranged to stay at the Seaman's Home where Ralph had stayed the previous year. I had to obtain visas for France and Britain and exchange my money for English pounds.

I had the pleasure of meeting the Guinter family on the White Star (if I recall the name of the ship correctly). It was a 20,000-ton liner of the Celtic line. The date was December 11, 1920, just over a year after Ralph had left New York. The Guinters had a young son named John, and I thoroughly enjoyed their company. They shared many insights about Africa with me, and I felt fortunate to travel alongside experienced individuals. Upon our arrival in Liverpool, we were greeted by Christian friends. Pastor Guinter and I took the train to London, where I vividly remember my first meal in the city—a breakfast of ham and eggs. I had some shopping to do there, particularly placing a large food order with Crosse and Blackwell, who specialized in shipping and packing items for tropical climates. I also acquired a tropical helmet. In addition to my practical tasks, I had the opportunity to do some sightseeing and visit friends of my brother Roy.

After our time in London, we returned to Liverpool to spend Christmas with the kind folks who had welcomed us upon our arrival. It was my first Christmas in a foreign land, far from my family, and I felt a tinge of loneliness. However, it was a blessed Christmas in a Christian home, and they had a daughter serving in the same part of Africa we were heading to. We shared in the joyous celebration together.

I believe it was December 29th when we embarked on the African steamer, which was noticeably smaller than the transatlantic ship we had previously traveled on. The voyage was fascinating, particularly when we emerged from the cold fog of the northern waters into the bright and sunny tropics.

Our first stop was at the Madeira Islands, followed by several ports along the West Coast. On January 9th, my 22nd birthday, I caught my first glimpse of the African shores near Dakar. It took a few more days before we reached Lagos, Nigeria. There, we were warmly received by the Secretary of the British and Foreign Bible Society, and we stayed in their home for several days as we made preparations for our journey inland.

The train initially took us through the tropical forest region and then onto a drier plateau with less vegetation. We disembarked at a river port, and the next day, we set off down the river to Lokoja. I distinctly remember that part of the journey because our boat got stuck on a sandbar, where it remained for several hours. Eventually, we arrived at Lokoja, where the Benue River merges with the Niger River. We spent several more days in a government rest-house while Mr. Guinter made all the necessary arrangements for our river journey. Ralph had traveled up the river from Lagos instead of taking the train, as we had done.

The boat trip was thrilling. The mission boat had been sent down to meet us. It was approximately 25 feet long and 6 feet wide, made of galvanized metal, and had a canopy with curtains that could be let down. Six men expertly maneuvered the boat using long poles, with four positioned in the front and two in the back. They would occasionally employ oars to navigate deeper sections of the river.

All our meals were prepared on the boat, with the cook managing a small fire at the back. Drinking water was taken directly from the river, though I didn't particularly enjoy it as it was cloudy and tasted smoky from being boiled over the wood fire. We would have our evening meal just before sundown and then set up camp for the night before darkness fell. Our camp beds and mosquito nets were set up on the sandbank, and a fire was kept burning throughout the night to ward off wild animals. This journey took place during the dry season, and we slept on the sandbank, sometimes half a mile away from the main riverbank due to high water levels.

I have never witnessed a river so abundant with diverse forms of life—human, animal, bird, and fowl. We often had fish as part of our meals, and at times Mr. Guinter would hunt ducks or geese. The river was populated with various species, including storks that would stand in the shallows to fish, pelicans, flamingoes, kingfishers, herons, and sandpipers, each of them unique. Hippos were present, although we were relieved to observe them from a distance. Ralph once shared an incident when nine hippos pursued his boat on the same river. It occurred during Ramadan, the fasting month for Muslims when they abstain from food during the day but feast at night. Ralph was eager to continue down the river swiftly, but his boatmen were sluggish and slow-paced. However, when the hippos chased them, they suddenly sped up to escape, successfully evading the hippos. Hippos are known to capsize boats, and many lives have been lost in such encounters.

The river was home to countless crocodiles. As we approached sandbanks, they would quickly slip into the water upon hearing the noise made by our boatmen. We often encountered dugout canoes carrying entire families, along with their animals, such as sheep, goats, chickens, and dogs. These people from downstream would travel upstream to fish, dry, smoke the fish, and then return home to sell them. Many of these individuals were followers of Islam, and we would hear the Muslim call to prayer after the roosters crowing just before dawn. I vividly recall hearing the roosters crowing and the call to prayer on the day Paul was born, March 12, 1922, in Ibi, Nigeria, on a Sunday morning. The roosters and the call to prayer awakened me, and that day held a significant call to action.

Roosters hold significance for Muslims during their travels. I remember one night when another family camped on the same sandbank. As they departed from the shore, I distinctly recall seeing the rooster being the last to board the boat. He had to jump several feet to make it aboard as the boat was leaving. He seemed to be accustomed to such leaps, as the people on board didn't seem concerned about him being left behind.

Numerous villages lined both sides of the river, and nearly every day, we would make stops to purchase items such as eggs, yams, chickens, and occasionally fresh meat.

During the day in the boat, I kept myself busy studying, sewing, and reading. The Guinters were kind enough to teach me the Hausa language, especially the household words, and how to adapt to living in the tropics and interacting with Africans. Their company and guidance were truly invaluable.

However, I couldn't help but wonder about Ralph's whereabouts. I hadn't received any word from him in Lagos but at Lokoja, a boy he had sent met us and joined our journey. On the very day we left New York, Ralph had embarked on a five-month trip from Garoua in Northern Cameroon. His purpose was to explore the region and seek where God wanted us to work. He traveled through areas inhabited by 20 tribes, where no missionaries had yet been.

Everywhere he went, Ralph was welcomed as a teacher sent from God. In one village, as he approached, he was greeted by several horsemen outside the town. Ralph thought they might be French officials welcoming him, but they rode up to him, stopped abruptly, turned around, and escorted him into town. Later, when he was taken to the chief's home, he was told, "Today you have come. We've been searching this road for the teacher who will teach us about God for five years. We have heard of God but don't know how to pray to Him." Ralph explained that he had come precisely to find such people, but he needed to return to his people first to share the news about the chief and his people, who were eager to learn. And so, he continued his journey. Whenever he had the opportunity, Ralph would preach the message of salvation wherever he stopped.

As Ralph ventured into the territory of Rey Bouba, an important chieftaincy in the region, he started receiving gifts from the chief even before reaching his town. Upon his arrival, he was warmly welcomed and invited to stay. He spent approximately a week there, engaging in conversations and sharing stories using a Bible picture roll, similar to what we use in Sunday Schools. A missionary from a different area had sent the picture roll to the chief.

During their interactions, Ralph mentioned to the chief that the Bible, or the Jesus-book as he called it, could also be found in his language, Arabic. The chief expressed his interest and made an intriguing offer. He said, "If you can get me the Jesus book in my tongue, I will give you a thousand francs." In those days, the franc held significant value, equivalent to saying, "I will give you a thousand dollars." Ralph humbly declined the offer of money but assured the chief that he would procure a copy of the book in Arabic and send it to him, which he later fulfilled.

In February 1921, the Guinters and I arrived in Ibi. I then traveled to Wukari, a station of the Sudan United Mission, where I would spend the next five months. My main focus during this time was the intensive study of the Hausa language, and I made good progress in acquiring it. Meanwhile, Mr. Guinter had gone up-country to construct houses in preparation for their upcoming work.

Mamita

While staying in Wukari, I resided with Mrs. Guinter. Our separate living arrangements didn't dampen our strong bond, and I would often join her for meals before retiring to my own little house nearby. During this time, the Guinters experienced the joy of welcoming a new member into their family—a precious baby girl. As a result, I took on the responsibility of managing the household and caring for little John. It was an invaluable experience that taught me so much.

Despite the initial exchange of one or two letters, a prolonged silence followed, leaving me increasingly unhappy and unsettled. The uncertainty gnawed at my heart, casting a shadow over my days in Wukari. Weeks turned into months, an agonizing wait, with no word from Ralph.

Then, one fateful night, as I lay in bed, rest eluding me, I heard the unmistakable sound of footsteps crunching on the gravel outside. It was June 8th, 1921—an evening shrouded in darkness. My senses heightened, anticipation filling the air. Ralph had arrived, his bicycle silently carrying him through the night from the distant town of Ibi to be reunited with me.

The emotions surged within me—relief, joy, and perhaps a hint of something more. Our meeting promised a renewed connection, an intertwining of our lives. Little did I know that this precious moment would forever mark a turning point in our journey, shaping our future in ways I could never have imagined.

Pregnancy and Birth of First Child (1922)

After enduring a separation of twenty long months since I bid farewell to Ralph at the Moline station, what a joyous reunion it was. The missionaries at Wukari shared in our delight as they listened eagerly to Ralph's report of his incredible journey. It was then that we made a decision—to retreat to a peaceful mountain rest-house. Ralph could dedicate time to writing his comprehensive report for the Mission Board in America in this sanctuary. The only challenge was that the rest-house was a daunting fifty miles away. We could rely on bicycles for transportation, but there was one problem—I had never learned to ride one.

With Ralph's patient guidance, I dedicated myself to mastering the art of riding a bicycle. It took a day of hard work and determination, but I eventually gained enough confidence to embark on our journey the following day. The scorching sun beat down upon us as we pedaled forward, traversing the dusty roads. I would dismount whenever we approached a bridge, cautious of the narrow footpath. Sprawling bushland rather than dense forests characterized this region of Northern Nigeria. Nevertheless, we pressed on without mishaps, arriving at our desired station by 4:00 p.m.

The warmth and hospitality Mrs. Malherbe, the missionary wife, extended to us will forever remain etched in my memory. In this sweltering climate, the custom among missionaries was to quench their thirst not with cold water but with hot tea. It may seem counterintuitive, but the hot tea was more refreshing in the scorching heat. I found myself indulging in five cups of the comforting brew.

In the warm embrace of our newfound friends, we were filled with a deep sense of belonging and comfort. During this time, we first met the nurse and midwife who would later play a crucial role in welcoming our son, Paul, into the world, nine months after that cherished reunion.

The next day, we set out on our journey. The men who accompanied us carried our supplies, camp furniture, food, and clothing as they traveled ahead throughout the day. They carried extra water, but Ralph and I had only one army canteen. Unfortunately, by the time we arrived at the base of the mountain, our water supply had run entirely out. I vividly remember our overwhelming thirst as we made our way up the mountain. It took us about an hour of strenuous climbing to reach the rest house, perched approximately a thousand feet above the surrounding plains.

The month spent at the rest house was fruitful, and once our report was completed, we made our way back to Wukari without any mishaps. That journey remains the first, last, and only time I have ridden a bicycle.

Now the question was, what would we do while waiting for the Mission Board's decision on our report? We knew it could take anywhere from 3 to 6 months. Mr. Guinter, the field director of the Sudan Mission, asked if we would be willing to go to Kona and help establish a station for the Sudan United Mission. He had already spent six weeks there and built living quarters. With no other immediate plans, we agreed to go to Kona. This meant another journey up the river, about a hundred miles, this time by a river steamer, which made the trip quicker. It was a true pioneer experience, but we found joy in our work there.

We encountered an unexpected reaction during one of our visits to a nearby village. When we arrived, the women and children ran away in fear, screaming. Later, we learned they had never seen a white woman before and thought I was a ghost. It was an amusing and memorable encounter.

During the early stages of my pregnancy, I experienced severe nausea, resulting in a weight loss of 25 pounds within six weeks. Ralph had previously visited a station of the Danish Mission further up the river. During his return journey from the interior, he finally received the telegram I had sent from Lagos back in January, which was the first news he had of my arrival in Nigeria.

Considering Ralph's prior knowledge of the Danish mission station, we traveled there for medical assistance. Thankfully, the doctor assured us that my condition was normal and that the nausea would soon subside. True to his words, I felt much better when we returned to Kona and could enjoy the remainder of our time there.

Each morning, we encountered sick individuals who sought our help, so our small dispensary gradually expanded. Additionally, we taught school, with Ralph instructing approximately 20 young men while I dedicated myself to caring for the younger boys.

Eventually, we needed to leave Kona and return to Ibi, as we were expecting our baby. It was the end of February, and the Guinters were coming to take over our responsibilities.

In Ibi, our son, Paul, was born on a Sunday morning, March 12, 1922. He was a healthy baby boy, weighing 9 1/2 pounds, and we were filled with gratitude and joy as parents.

MAMITA'S JOURNAL OF PAUL'S BABYHOOD (1921-1922)

December 11th 1921

To Our Little Sunbeam:

You are with us. God has blessed us and given us you. We have not yet seen your face but, as each day goes by, we are learning to know you. How happy your father and I were when we first realized that you were at last on your way to us. For years we have both looked forward to welcoming you. Though we have failed many times and fallen far short yet our ideals have always been such as this: "I want to live such a life as God would have me live, such a life that a son or daughter of mine might not be ashamed of, and moreover, such a life as might prove a help, not a hindrance, to any child God might entrust to my care." Early in the lives of both of us, God implanted the desire in us to become parents. Early in young womanhood it became clear to me that the greatest thing I, or any woman could be, would be to be a mother. Since then I have longed for you, I have prayed for you, I have loved you. And so it was with your father. Fatherhood meant and means to him one of the most sacred blessings God can bestow upon man. And, as I've said, though we feel that we have fallen far short of what God would have us be, our prayer has continually been, and always will be-"God, help us to become real parents if Thou dost entrust the nurture of children to us. We want to be co-workers of thine, instruments of Thine that Thou mayest be glorified."

Why am I writing this? Only because I want to commune with you. It will be years hence before you read these words, if ever, but I want you to know that we welcome you as one of Gods richest blessings, and we are so happy to have you with us.

Mamita

It was on October 16th that you first made your presence known to us. That morning it seemed I was not feeling very well. I also felt very heavy in spirit. I lay down a few minutes to rest. But what was that? Strange stirrings beneath my heart! Ah! Sunbeam, tack, tack, you were a sunbeam then. An unspeakable joy came over me. I forgot my tiredness and could only rejoice and praise God. Then, if not before, you became a living personality to me. I could hardly wait for your father to come into the noon meal for eagerness to tell him the good news. And when he hears it his heart was made glad and in the words of David we joined in praise-"bless the Lord, 0 my soul, Who satisfieth thy desire with good things so that thy youth is renewed like the eagle." Since then not a day has passed but you have made yourself known, and many a time have you served as a sunbeam to us. Sometimes you become quite vigorous in your expressions so that I must laugh and rejoice.

These are quiet days, but happy ones for they are our first days together in our own humble home, sweet home, together. After years of longing for a home of one's own, even long before we knew each other (and it is now five years since our life paths first crossed), at last we are enjoying that privilege of laboring together, and that of all the daily joys of true love. It is a quiet life, I say, for we are far from all dear ones. We only have two white neighbors whom we seldom see. But we are enjoying our home life in two little mud huts, our labors and life among these black brothers and sisters. There is great joy and satisfaction in it for we feel God's presence with us in this work. There is joy in doing the humble tasks that each new day brings.

We are enjoying our books which we have for such a long time wanted to become better acquainted with. The Good book is more and more becoming the living Word. We cannot quench our thirst for study but each day finds us longing for more. Truly this surpasses school day education. Sometimes school study is "study because one has to," although I always enjoyed my school work. Each autumn found me longing for school to open.

Yes, these are quiet days. They are peaceful days. How we do enjoy our walks every evening. We have some beautiful wild paths. We are in a little valley surrounded by mountains. We enjoy them, but we also enjoy the broad expanse of the plain which we cannot see unless we go around or over the mountain. On Sunday evening after tea we discovered a path winding around the mountain. From this we could see a beautiful view of plain, of valley, and of mountains piled up in the distance. What a happy discovery! Since then we often find ourselves following that path, especially when we feel the need of the atmosphere of the broadening plain. On the days which have been particularly nerve-trying we find ourselves following the path that leads to a shady, cool spot where a little stream incessantly murmurs and gurgles

"For men may come and men may go / But I go on forever."

Here there are wide spreading trees in whose branches there are always many birds.

Today, Sunday, December 11 being an anniversary of Father's leaving Garua for his long eastward trek in almost unknown lands, as well as the anniversary of my sailing from New York, we wished to commemorate these events in some fitting way. With a book, "Quiet Talks on Home Ideals" by S. D. Gordon in hand we found the waterside-the gurgling brook whose murmurings are such sweet music to our ears. In the trees by the brook Nature has provided a very comfortable rustic seat where Father insisted I should sit. He found a seat on a nearby log.

Your name, if a boy, is to be Paul Daniel. These months we have been carefully studying the epistles and life of St. Paul. Because we admire this servant of God so much we should like to have a son by that name. Daniel is one of your father's names, and the name of his grandfather.

Mamita

If you are a girl your name is to be Dorothy Pauline. Dorothy-a gift of God.

February 24th, 1922. We leave our little home and our friends in the valley. When and where will our next home be? We have a very trying day. Capt. Fitzpatrick says we must not walk through Lau because of the small-pox there. That means we have to follow a bush-path to the river. Our loads get ahead of us. We have only a few cookies and one bottle of water. It is dusk before we finally reach our loads. Ralph was so thirsty his tongue clove to the roof of his mouth. We had thought to meet the Gunters here but do not.

February 25th. Early this a.m. the Gunters come to our stopping place. We have an hour with them. How good it does seem to see them again! How glad we are that they are to carry on the work at Kwona until the Olsons arrive. This is another bad day. We are misled. The swamp grass is so high that I must get out of the hammock and mount the horse. We find ourselves quite a way down stream from Kwatan Muri and the only way of getting there is to follow a dry bed of the river which is very, very sandy. We finally come to the steep bank and I become exhausted. Father leaves me with Shumen and goes on with another man. He soon finds Kwatan Muri and brings a canoe. Oh! How thankful we are but so tired. We finally arrive at Kwatan Muri and find the old Mission Barge.

February 26th. We start our journey on the river. We have all our meals in the barge. We camp on the sandbank at night. One night a hyena runs around our beds. After a favorable journey we arrive in Ibi on -

March 4th. We are at the Mission Station before the Farrants realize we have come. We are warmly received. The bungalow which father helped to build when he first arrived in Africa is to be our home. We find it quite luxurious with all its cupboards, dressers,

109

tables, beds, chairs, bathroom and real doors and windows. Miss Vosloo has not yet arrived. But things for the little wardrobe which had come from Montgomery Ward were here. We are taking our meals with the Farrants.

March 11th [1922]. I have a premonition that the big day is at hand. So everybody gets busy. The little bed is prepared. It is a basket from a bathtub which Father fixes up. Mrs. Farrant and Miss Vosloo are helping with the bed clothes and the mosquito net. I have a good night's rest. I awaken at 3 a.m., hear the cocks crow and soon afterward the Mohammedan call to prayer, but I sleep on until 6 o'clock.

March 12th. At 6 o'clock I call Miss Vosloo to tell her I think something is about to happen. I go in to Father's room to tell him. Miss Vosloo expects me to take breakfast but there's no time for that. For two hours Miss Vosloo and Father are very busy. Finally, a few minutes before 9 o'clock you arrive - you - Paul Daniel, our son, our sunbeam.

Where did you come from, baby dear? / Out of the everywhere into the here. / Where did you get your eyes so blue? / Out of the sky as I came through. / What makes the light in them sparkle and spin? / Some of the starry spikes left in.

March 13th. The day after your arrival, dear Paul, the joy in the house is palpable. Miss Vosloo and Mrs. Farrant come to visit and they marvel at how strong and alert you are. Father can hardly stop smiling, his eyes twinkling with the same light I see in yours. He holds you in his arms and I see a new tenderness in him that I haven't seen before. You have brought a new dimension to our lives.

March 15th. Life in Ibi continues. Your Father and I are busy making our little bungalow a real home for you. Your tiny clothes from Montgomery Ward are adorable. We have also received a package of toys and books for you from a kind missionary family in

Mamita

Johannesburg. Father and I spend the evening reading the books and playing with the toys, imagining the day when you will be able to join us.

March 20th. You are one week old today, little Paul! You are so tiny, yet so strong and determined. I see in you the same resolve your Father and I have to make the most of our life here. Your Father has taken to calling you his 'little explorer', a title you seem to embrace as you survey your new world with wide-eyed wonder.

March 24th. Father has been working tirelessly to make our home more comfortable. He's built a small veranda where we can sit in the evenings and enjoy the cool breeze. He's also built a cradle for you. It's simple, but made with such love and care that it's more precious to me than any store-bought one could be.

April 1st. We're becoming accustomed to the rhythms of life here. The days are filled with simple pleasures - meals together, walks along the river, quiet moments with you, Paul. The community has been welcoming and we are thankful for their kindness. We are learning the local language, bit by bit, so that we can communicate better with our neighbors.

April 5th. Father and I are continuing our studies of the Good Book. We want to instill in you the same love for learning and discovery that we have. We hope that one day, you will be able to read these words and understand the love and hope we have for you.

April 10th. The heat of the day is becoming more intense, but the nights remain cool and refreshing. We take you out in the evenings to feel the cool breeze on your tiny face. You seem to enjoy it and it helps you sleep through the night.

April 15th. Easter Sunday. We celebrate the resurrection of Jesus with a small service in our home. Father leads the prayer and I sing a hymn, while you sleep peacefully in your cradle. Despite the distance from our families and the familiarity of our previous Easter traditions, this Easter is special because it's your first.

As the days pass, dear Paul, you grow stronger and more alert. Each day, you bring us joy and a renewed sense of purpose. You are our sunbeam, lighting up our lives with your innocence and love. We are so thankful for the gift of you, and we pray that we may be worthy of this great blessing God has bestowed upon us.

Typoscript. Excerpts.

Leaving for East Africa

While in Kona, after months of waiting, we received a communication from the Mission Board inquiring if we would be willing to go to Tanganyika. The Leipzig Mission had appealed to the National Lutheran Council, seeking American Lutherans to continue their work in Tanganyika. The German missionaries were repatriated after the war ended, and Tanganyika transitioned from a German colony to an English mandate.

Despite Ralph's detailed report of his lengthy trip, the Mission Board did not provide any acknowledgment. Instead, they simply asked us to respond with a cable stating "yes" or "no" regarding our willingness to go to Tanganyika. However, we couldn't send a simple yes or no response. Therefore, our cable stated: "Yes, Need Justifying Change."

Two weeks after the birth of our son Paul, we received the cable informing us to proceed to Tanganyika. It arrived on a Sunday, and by the following Wednesday, we departed from Ibi by boat to embark on this new journey.

CONFLICTS BETWEEN THE MISSION BOARD AND THE SUDAN UNITED MISSION

[Shortly before Ralph departed for his first trip to Africa in 1919, during his final meeting with Dr. Kumm, he becomes aware of the long-standing divide between the Mission Board and the Sudan United Mission (S.U.M.). Dr. Brandelle, representing the Board at the meeting with the S.U.M. in Princeton, sent the telegram asking Ralph to abandon his work in Nigeria (considered to be part of Sudan by the S.U.M.) and relocate to Tanzania immediately, shattering Ralph's vision and plans.]

10/21 [1919] Find Dr. Brandelle already at Princeton when I come and my good friend from Hartford, Harold Austin, who has come to be presented as a candidate for the S.U.M. – We wait in the reading room of Murray Dodge Hall till a few minutes before the close of the session of the Council when we are brought into the room where it has been in session. A short season of prayer closes the meeting. -- I leave the room questioning myself as to whether or not it has been worth the time and expense for Dr. Brandelle and myself to come all this way for those few minutes. – We have a bite to eat and then run for the train. Dr. Kumm invites me to go with him to Summit, but I decide to go on to New York to call on cousin Viola. – I spend an hour with her. We are thinking of Martin. She takes his latest address so as to write to him at once,

113

hoping to get to see him when he returns. – Spend the night in the Reading Room at the Immigrant Home.

10/22 Out to Summit. As I cross the Hudson by Ferry my thoughts are again with Martin. God bring our brother safely back home soon. – At Summit, Dr. Kumm proposes a walk. Such a fine morning for a walk. The doctor has a purpose. If I understand him correctly, he has no sympathy with our idea of a Lutheran Mission in the Sudan. He tells me of the trouble "**these Norwegians and Danes**" are giving the S.U.M. **All this sounds most discouraging to me. Had our people in 1917 heard such talk, would they have resolved to take up work in the Sudan? I believe not.** When that resolution was passed, it was taken for granted that we should have a field of our own. That has been my impression all the time, and I have tried my best to make that clear at all times in my dealings with the Board and with Dr. Kumm. Our relations with the S.U.M. should be only a very general cooperation, not an affiliation. This whole matter may appear in a different light when I reach the field, but now I certainly cannot favor an affiliation. – After dinner, we prepare a list of things for my outfit. This list is prepared from an Englishman's point of view and will no doubt be altered by the habits and tastes of an American. Had Dr. K. lived and labored for any length of time on the field [Is Ralph questioning K. advice? The typescript has no punctuation mark here.] – **In spite of our very decided differences of opinion on some matters, how I do admire Dr. Kumm!** He is a man of contrasts: almost domineering and still desirous to serve his fellows.

Quoted from a typoscript: Two Years in the Life of Ralph Hult. Excerpts from diaries, 1917 and 1919. Edited by Adeline Hult. 1991.

Frau Gertrud Trobisch

Martin Trobisch (1921)

In 1921 the time came when my teaching profession and personal life intertwined. After four years of military service and three years of French prison camp, Martin Trobisch finally returned to his old school, the 31st District School, at Easter 1921. He found it challenging to reintegrate into school life, especially as pedagogy was beginning to take new paths during that time. However, having been trained in these latest insights and experiences, I was able to help ease his transition back into teaching. During long walks, we discussed various problems and, in the process, got to know and love each other. In October 1921, we became engaged and spent the Christmas holidays at his parents' house in Bautzen.

Martin's father, Moritz Trobisch, was born on March 19, 1856, in Grävenitz, Saxony. His father was the owner of a windmill. After completing his mandatory schooling, Moritz joined the military and served for 12 years. He left the military as a non-commissioned officer and obtained a civil service position as a chief constable at the Bautzen Regional Court. Initially, his office was located in the Ortenburg, the castle above Bautzen. In 1885, he married Clara Wehner. Her

115

parents owned a small inn in Niederkaina near Bautzen. They came from the Sorbian region, and Martin's mother was fluent in the Sorbian language. That's how I remember her.

THE SORBIAN NATION

The Sorbs, also known as the Wends, are a Slavic minority living mainly in the region of Lusatia in eastern Germany. The term "Wends" dates to Roman historians who used "Veneti" to refer to unknown eastern tribes, later becoming "Wenden" in German. Both terms, Sorbs and Wends, are used interchangeably.

Sorbian is a West Slavic language. The ancestors of today's Sorbs/Wends were originally Slavic tribes from the northeast of the Carpathian Mountains who settled in the area between the Baltic Sea and the Erzgebirge about 1500 years ago.

In the early 19th century, Sorbs/Wends lived predominantly in rural villages with limited industrial influence. However, many of them migrated to cities during this time, often leading to a loss of their Sorbian-Wendish identity.

During the 19th century, the Sorbs faced societal challenges and were not always treated as equals. The emergence of the nation-state and the formation of the German Empire in 1871 led to a dominant German language and culture, putting pressure on Sorbian language and culture. As a result, many Sorbs had to conceal their identity or assimilate to avoid discrimination.

This pressure intensified during the Nazi regime, which actively sought to eradicate the Sorbian national identity.

Historically, the Sorbs have been traditionally associated with the Catholic Church. While the Reformation gained significant support in Saxony, the Lutheran doctrine spread throughout the region, impacting the preservation of Catholic traditions among the Sorbs.

Engagement, Wedding (1922)

Martin Johannes was born on October 14, 1888. He was a frail child. Since his mother had whooping cough, he was born with it, which initially caused his parents a lot of worry. However, he grew up to be a very calm and agreeable child. When he played with his building blocks, he preferred to hide under a table so that no one could knock them down. After elementary school, he attended the practical school associated with Bautzen's teacher training college. In 1910, he passed the final exam. After two years as an assistant teacher in Taubenheim an der Spree, he passed the second teacher's examination and was appointed as a provisional teacher in Leipzig. He joined the 31st District School.

On my 29th birthday, during Pentecost in 1922, we got married, and from then on, we walked to our school together every day. We lived with my mother. There was space for us in her apartment because my sister Marie had married in 1921. Her husband had studied Mathematics and Physics in Leipzig and was now a teacher in Eibenstock in the Erzgebirge region. Unfortunately, he succumbed to a severe flu after a short marriage.

During this time, the state began its campaign against double earners. All married female teachers were terminated upon payment of a severance package. However, we Gaudig students had not attended the school "for the development of personality" in vain. We joined forces in the "Association of Married Female Teachers" and fought for our rights. Since the years of service during the war counted twice, we already had more than ten years of service and were eligible for a pension. Those who refused to accept termination and the severance package were put on a waiting allowance. We received a certain monthly amount of about a hundred marks, but we had to be ready to take on substitute teaching for an absent colleague at any given time.

COAT OF ARMS TROBISCH FAMILY (1640-1888)

1640

The farmer Michael Trobisch emigrated from Moravia in Austria due to religious persecution. He briefly stayed in Lusatia, but then purchased a farm in Pieschen near Dresden. This information can be found in the land registry office in Dresden Neustadt.

1675

His son Andreas Trobisch took over the family estate. His son Johann went to war against the Turks with Elector Georg and participated with distinction in the Battle of Vienna in 1683. Upon his return, he took over

1698

the family estate. The eldest son trained as a carpenter, later became a master carpenter, and together with the architects Pöppelmann and Bähr built the Heilige Dreikoenigskirche [Holy Three Kings Church] in Dresden. The year of construction was 1732. He also took over the family estate. A younger brother named Hans, born on 3rd September

1701

bought a farm in Grossdoberitz near Meissen. [...] Hans Tobisch was a farmer and presiding judge, he died on June 17, 1776.

The old family coat of arms showed a leaping wolf in a blue field. Hans Trobisch changed the coat of arms to standardize the spelling of T and D. Instead of the wolf, he placed a T, under which two hands clasped together as a sign, indicating what a Trobisch promises by handshake is as good as an oath to him. The oak branch around the shield represents strength. Above the shield, the rising sun with the year 1640 symbolizes the year when

119

the name Trobisch was mentioned for the first time. Above the sun, the citizen's crown is a sign that the Trobisch have always shown themselves to be honorable among their fellow men. The motto on the crown says that a Trobisch always submits to the will of his God. He begins his daily work with the words: "Let God rule." Below the shield, the farming tools show that the Trobisch have grown up in agriculture.

This presiding judge Hans Trobisch in Grossdoberitz had a son born on 25th December

1740

named Johann Christian. He bought a farm in Jessen near Meissen and [...] died on February 20, 1800, from an epidemic disease. In the church book, he is recorded as a good, dignified man. Johann Christian Trobisch had triplets born on 24th April

1784

a son with two deceased daughters. The son, Johann Gottlob, later took over the family business in Jessen [...]. He sustained a crush injury during a house construction, leading to his death on May 25, 1834. [...] His eldest son Johann Gotthelf Trobisch, born on 26th August

1807

[...] was a farmer in Nünchritz near Riesa, he died on July 28, 1885. [...]

The birth certificate of the author of these lines reads: Wilhelm Moritz Trobisch, as the legitimate sixth child of the estate owner Johann Gotthelf Trobisch, born on 19th March

1858

in Nünchritz near Riesa. Since 1879 in Bautzen. He first served in the military for three years, Infantry Regiment Number 103, then

Mutti

41 years at the district court in Bautzen, lastly 15 years as a chief constable. Retired since 1923. Married on June 22, 1885, to Clara Wehnert, born on November 8, 1866, in Bautzen. She was the daughter of the innkeeper Moritz Wehnert in Niederkaina near Bautzen, born on January 13, 1821, in Bautzen, died on February 2, 1889, in Bautzen. Moritz Wehnert was married to Magdalena Sperling, born as the daughter of the business owner Andreas Sperling on March 14, 1829, in Nadelwitz near Bautzen, died on April 1, 1878, in Niederkaina. From the marriage of Wilhelm Moritz Trobisch, there were six children: Artur, born April 18, 1886, Magdalene, born June 10, 1887, **Martin [Mutti's husband], born October 14, 1888**, Hedwig, born May 18, 1892, Johannes, born January 15, 1897, Max, born April 3, 1899. Magdalene died in childhood. Artur fell in the World War in 1914.

All ancestors were baptized Lutheran.

Source: Typoscript with handwritten corrections.

[The last sentence is telling. During the Nazi regime, the pressure to eradicate the Sorbian national identity intensified greatly. Historically, the Sorbs have been associated with the Catholic Church. However, due to the spread of Lutheran doctrine in the region, the Sorbs faced challenges in preserving their Catholic traditions. Mutti's father-in-law, Moritz, the author of this family history, was married to a Sorbian woman, Clara, but he seems to try to downplay the family's Sorbian and Catholic connections by insisting that "all ancestors were baptized Lutheran." Pieschen near Dresden, where Michael Trobisch lived in 1640, is a Catholic Sorbian settlement. – Ironically, "Trobisch" might be of Sorbian origin; the Sorbian "drob" refers to fragmented or small pieces, and "ic" is a diminutive suffix in Slavic languages, adding a sense of familiarity or intimacy to a word: "dear little one."]

121

MOTHERHOOD (1923-1927)

Mamita

Douala. Boma. Loanda.

We traveled by boat from Lokoja on the Benue River, then down the Niger River to the head of the railway, and finally took a train to Lagos. It took us some time in Lagos to make arrangements for our journey to Tanganyika. The British and Foreign Bible Society Secretary and his wife advised us to return to England and travel through the Mediterranean Sea and the Red Sea. They felt it was safer, considering we had our baby with us, rather than taking the risky trip south and around the West Coast. Boat services along the West Coast were uncertain due to the presence of British, Spanish, French, and Portuguese colonies with limited inter-coastal trade. However, despite the risks, Ralph and I were determined to see Africa and visit missions along the way. Ralph would have preferred to travel overland if he were alone.

Our chosen route was as follows: we boarded a side-wheeler steamer from Lagos to Dahome on the Lagoon. From there, we took a French steamer to Douala. We met French Protestant missionaries on the boat who invited us to stay with them in Douala, Cameroon. So, Paul and I stayed with them while Ralph visited the Presbyterian Mission up-country, including Elat (where Ingrid's son was born last year

[1958]), and other stations. During our time in Douala, I had the opportunity to attend a French wedding, witnessing the marriage of a lady missionary who had arrived on our boat to a young missionary who had been there for a year. Before leaving Douala, we had Paul vaccinated by the mission's director, also a doctor. He considered it risky for us to travel with such a young, unvaccinated baby in an area with a high incidence of smallpox.

Continuing our journey, we boarded a French boat and disembarked at Boma in the Congo. Unfortunately, this was where we had an unhappy experience. The American missionaries of the Christian and Missionary Alliance in Boma refused to accommodate us in their home, so we had to find lodging at a hotel. I remember our anxious Sunday in our hotel room with a sick baby, but thankfully Paul recovered. It turned out that his illness was a reaction to the vaccination, so we knew the cause, even though there wasn't much we could do to help him.

We proceeded further up the river to Matadi, which only took a few hours. Matadi had a couple of mission stations, including one from the Swedish Covenant Church. From Boma, we boarded a small ocean steamer named "Wall" that would take us to Loanda in Portuguese West Africa, just a few hours away. Unfortunately, both Ralph and I experienced seasickness on the boat.

The Methodists warmly received us in Loanda, and we spent over a week there. They welcomed us with open arms. One of the Methodist families was preparing to travel to South Africa due to health reasons. The wife and one of the children had previously contracted Bubonic Plague and were not in good health. Loanda is an old town with historical significance. It was the place where Livingstone arrived from the inland and received letters from home. We also met the first American Consul in Africa, allowing us to register Paul's birth officially.

Capetown

From Loanda, we embarked on a German boat bound for Capetown, and the journey took us eight days. Although it could have been a comfortable and pleasant trip, Ralph suffered from severe toothache. He had broken a tooth some time ago, likely due to small rocks in the beans. On the bright side, Paul was a growing baby, adapting well to travel.

We were accommodated at a Mission Home during our stay in Capetown, which we deeply appreciated as it allowed us to cook our own meals again. We consulted with a doctor, Dr. Moffatt, who was the grandson of a pioneer missionary. He advised us to stay in Capetown for at least six months. Following his recommendation, we moved to a Christian rest home in a country village near Capetown. There, we experienced rapid improvement in our health. We were treated exceptionally well, receiving hot milk every night at nine o'clock and being served coffee in bed every morning. We met fascinating individuals and enjoyed the excellent climate.

During our time in Capetown, Ralph diligently worked on his report and a map of his trip. He distributed numerous copies to Mission Headquarters in Europe and America, fearing we might not return to the Sudan. He felt it was important to pass on the challenge of this journey to others. Years later, while aboard the Zamzam, Ralph encountered missionaries from the Norwegian Mission who mentioned that Ralph's report had initially directed their attention to the region of Africa where they were currently serving.

Tanganyika (1923-1926)

After spending four and a half months in the Cape, the doctor deemed us healthy enough to continue our journey. Along the way, we made a stop in Durban for a few days. Durban is renowned as a popular health resort along the southeast coast. Once again, we visited a Swedish Mission and stayed at another Mission Rest Home.

We arrived at Tanga after making stops at Zanzibar and Dar-es-salaam. From Tanga, we boarded a train that took us to Moshi. Pastor Zeilinger greeted us there, and we proceeded to Old Moshi, where Mrs. Zeilinger welcomed us and provided us with a home. We stayed in Old Moshi for several weeks while awaiting our designated station. We were finally assigned to Machame, at the foot of Mount Kilimanjaro.

Alexander Eisenschmidt

During that time, we had the pleasure of meeting Leipzig missionaries, including Pastor Alexander Eisenschmidt, who was allowed to continue his work due to his Estonian heritage. He had been overseeing the work at Machame, although he resided a couple of hours away. I remember the words he wrote in our guest book, as he was our first guest in our East African home: "Yea, the sparrow hath found an house, and the swallow a nest for herself, where she may lay her young, even at thine altars, O Lord of hosts, my King and my God" (Psalm 84:3).

Machame and Moshi

Ralph's diary contains detailed accounts of our four years in Tanganyika, so that I won't delve into them further. It wasn't until Paul was ten months old that we had our own home in January 1923. Our initial two years were devoted to Machame and the subsequent two years in Moshi. It was an incredibly busy and challenging period for Ralph as the field director. He faced numerous issues and had to undertake extensive travel. During his ten-week absence while visiting Iramba and the Dar-es-salaam area, Paul and I were left on our own at home.

The return of the German missionaries posed a significant challenge as the Leipzig Mission and Augustana had to negotiate the division of the field. Ultimately, when the German missionaries arrived, they were assigned to Machame, and we were reassigned to Moshi. It was the first time we shared a station with others. This change meant that when Ralph had to be away, I had the support and companionship of fellow missionaries. During this time, our family continued to grow, and John became an integral part of our lives. Shortly before we departed for the United States, our joy expanded with the birth of our daughter Ingrid on February 17, 1926.

But before our departure, we had one last stop in Machame. We planned to spend Sunday there to witness the dedication of their new church. When we first arrived in Machame, the congregation, consisting of 600 members, worshipped in a small mud church that was far too cramped for their needs. However, piles of rocks surrounded the church, collected by the Christians as they aspired to build a new place of worship. Unfortunately, the war forced the missionaries to leave, causing the congregation to lose hope and abandon the project.

It was Ralph who reignited their passion. He encouraged them to take matters into their own hands and reminded them that they had skilled stone cutters and masons among them. Now, after four years of hard work, the construction of the grand stone building was almost complete. With a seating capacity of 2,000 people, it is one of the largest churches in East Africa. I consider it a true testament to Ralph's dedication, as without his challenge and assistance, it would not have been realized—at least not at that time. Today, the congregation has grown to an astonishing 12,000 people.

During our time in Machame, we witnessed memorable baptism ceremonies. Two hundred twenty-five adults were baptized on one Sunday, followed by around 60 of their young children the following Sunday. The area was densely populated, with approximately ten out-schools serving as chapels and preaching centers. These out-schools have since grown into smaller churches, all contributing to the larger congregation. Ralph had the honor of baptizing and officiating the wedding of a young chief who has become one of Africa's most influential leaders. Some individuals from this region have even visited the United States or pursued education there. One notable example is a young man who graduated from Bethany College and now holds a prominent position in the government. The Chagga people have always been known for their progressive mindset, and many have achieved wealth through their prosperous coffee plantations.

The dedication service became our farewell as we prepared to leave Africa.

Mutti

Alexander Eisenschmidt

Alexander Eisenschmidt, or "Eisi" as we used to call him when he helped my mother take care of us children after my father had passed away, was called by the Leipzig Mission Society to serve as a missionary in British East Africa in 1908. I vividly recall attending the church service at the Nikolaikirche in Leipzig when his assignment was celebrated. It was an emotional and impactful moment, witnessing the sending-off ceremony. However, at that time, I had no personal thoughts or desires in my 15-year-old heart. Little did I know that Eisenschmidt had developed deeper feelings for me over the years, seeing me not as "one of the three sisters" but as the one he loved most and intended to marry. He had hoped to take a leave in 1915, when I turned 22, to come to Leipzig, marry me, and bring me to Estonia. However, he never shared this plan with me.

Although Eisenschmidt wrote me numerous letters, which I thoroughly enjoyed reading, especially his descriptions of his travels to Mount Kilimanjaro and Lake Victoria, I never saw him as anything more than a friend. During my time as a private tutor at Rittergut Liebau in 1913, he consistently included a hyphen in

131

the address "Lieb—au"? ["Lieb" is German for "love"]. Perhaps his attempts at courtship were too subtle, and I never gave them much consideration. It didn't bother me much when the First World War disrupted his plans and kept him in Africa for another seven years. At that time, I had my own ambitions of becoming a teacher, and marriage was not a priority for me.

When we were children, Eisenschmidt engaged in a lengthy conversation with Muttel during one of his visits. He always carried a walking stick, a constant companion due to his condition, and would lean it against the garden gate. One day, my little sister and I mischievously took the stick and adorned it with colorful glass beads, hoping to annoy or tease him. To our surprise, Eisenschmidt collected all the beads with care. Then, in 1924, after a long separation, he presented me with a colorful glass bead ring that he had made from those same beads.

Alexander Eisenschmidt married the widow of a missionary and became a stepfather to her eldest son, Rudolf Mauer. When the Eisenschmidts returned to Africa, Rudolf joined our family and lived in our home for several years. He completed his education in Germany but felt a strong connection to Africa. Following a brief period as a teacher, he ventured to work on a coffee farm in southern East Africa. However, with the onset of World War II, Rudolf returned to

Germany and enlisted in the German army. Tragically, he gave up his young life on a battlefield in France.

Children. End of Teaching career (1923-1927)

Our oldest child Walter was born on November 29, 1923. It was a time of inflation, and we had very little money. So, we were very grateful that the boy was born in November, as we could use the child benefit paid for the current month. On December 1, Martin received part of his salary in the stable currency for the first time, the so-called Rentenmark of that time. This allowed him to pay the midwife in such currency for her efforts. I will never forget her radiant face.

Still in Muttel's apartment, our second child, Hertha, was born on May 10, 1925. It was a beautiful, warm May night, and the girl only took three hours to enter this world.

Martin had learned shorthand, specifically Gabelsberger shorthand, and obtained a teaching certification in stenography. After the introduction of the universal shorthand system, he sacrificed his summer vacation in 1926 to relearn it. We were in Zempin on the island of Usedom, and I remember that I had to dictate to him in the evenings with a stopwatch while the children were asleep.

My situation as a substitute teacher became unbearable in the summer of 1926. Our son Walter was two and a half years old, and Hertha was just one year old. We had moved into our own apartment by then. Since I needed someone for the children and also assistance for the household, my waiting allowance was not enough to pay for these helpers. It did not seem fair that Martin had to contribute from his income so I could go and work as a teacher. After completing my substitute period, I decided to end this situation and "go all-in," as they say. I wrote to the authorities that I couldn't continue working under these conditions. I needed a salary that corresponded to my years of service. If they couldn't pay that, I requested my retirement. I am still amazed today, but I received the following response: "Based on § 14 of the Personnel Reduction Act of January 29, 1924, you will be retired as of July 31, 1927." Now we had our peace and an additional monthly pension of a hundred marks. I was 34 years old at the time. When the mailman delivered my pension for the first time, and I opened the door, he asked, astonished, "Where is the retiree?" Sometimes Martin jokingly said that he didn't realize he was getting such a good deal when he married me.

RAISING A FAMILY (1927-1939)

Mamita

Trip to New York

We departed from Moshi and embarked on a train journey to Tanga. Upon our arrival, we found ourselves waiting for a few days in a hotel. The heat in Tanga was unbearable, and water was scarce. We were only allowed a small amount of water for bathing and had to rely on soda water for drinking. Despite the discomfort of the prickly heat, we managed to stay in good health.

Around the time of Paul's fourth birthday in March 1926, we boarded a German boat bound for Hamburg. The journey took us five weeks, providing a much-needed period of rest for us all. Ralph had been tirelessly working throughout our time in East Africa. The trip through the Red Sea was sweltering, but the remainder of the voyage was pleasant. The boat served as both a freighter and a passenger vessel, and we had the opportunity to meet other missionaries on board.

Our route included a stop in Genoa, where we could disembark for a day. We enjoyed a lovely car trip along the Riviera, soaking in the scenic beauty. Departing early on Easter morning, with the church bells ringing, we remained within sight of the shore throughout the forenoon. I distinctly recall the gambling casino being pointed out to us. Our next stop was Marseille, where we took a horse and buggy ride through the town. We had a brief stop in Malaga, Spain, and although the boat stopped at Lisbon, we remained on board as passengers were not allowed to go ashore. It was from Lisbon that Ralph would embark on a boat for the United States approximately 15 years later, after his Zamzam experience.

The boat stopped at Southampton, the port of London, but passengers could not disembark. Our next stop was Rotterdam, where, as we sailed up the river, we were greeted by the beautiful sight of tulip fields in full bloom on both sides. One of the most memorable experiences of that day was a visit to the zoo, considered one of the finest in the world.

Upon our arrival in Hamburg, we spent a few days there, arranging our journey to Sweden. During our stay, we found accommodation in a private hostel. Our original plan was to continue to Sweden, as fellow missionaries on the boat had informed us about a rest home for missionaries in Tyrings, southern Sweden. We decided that I spend five weeks there with the children in March 1926 while Ralph traveled back to visit Mission Headquarters in Berlin, Leipzig, Bielefeld, and other cities. He also made stops in Copenhagen, Paris, and London. It was a delightful time of the year, and I thoroughly enjoyed experiencing the

Swedish springtime. Meals were provided, so my primary responsibility was looking after the children. The boys especially enjoyed playing outdoors, and I found great peace of mind knowing that I didn't have to worry about amoebas from playing in the dirt or the risk of sunstroke if they lost their hats. As we journeyed from Portugal, we witnessed spring's arrival and our first sighting of lilacs.

Our return voyage home was aboard the Stavangerfjord, a Norwegian liner. They offered to cover our train fare from Malmo to Oslo and our hotel in Oslo, as they were competing with the Swedish line. This allowed us to see more of both Sweden and Norway. During our Atlantic crossing, we encountered icebergs. For approximately three days, we traveled slowly in dense fog, with the sound of the foghorn accompanying us constantly. Then, one afternoon, we emerged into the bright sunlight, providing a great sense of relief. However, we spotted a colossal mountain-like iceberg to our side and not far away. After that, our journey progressed smoothly.

It was thrilling to enter New York Harbor. Since the Synod was in session in Philadelphia, we headed directly there. If my memory serves me right, we arrived on a Saturday. I had a severe toothache, so we had to locate a dentist and have my tooth extracted on a Sunday.

Mamita

Arriving in Missouri

Weinhardt, who had hoped to go to the Sudan with our church, became ordained that year. Over the next two years, he and Ralph frequently met at Board meetings as Ralph also desired to return to the Sudan. However, when the Board ultimately decided to focus solely on Tanganyika, Weinhardt went to the Sudan with Gunderson. During their time there, marked by challenges to their health, Weinhardt started contemplating and praying for Mission work in South America and Asia. As you know, he eventually became one of the first missionaries of the World Mission Prayer League in Bolivia.

My brother Roy and his wife Dorothy met us in Chicago, and we stayed at their apartment, conveniently located near the University of Chicago campus. Coincidentally, Dorothy was graduating from the University of Chicago on that day. One of our first tasks together was to go out and purchase a dress for me to attend her graduation ceremony. It was a wonderful experience to cross the United States in June after being away for so many years.

Arriving in Colona and finding Mother and Father settled in their new home brought immense joy to our hearts. From there, we proceeded to Wahoo, where Mother Hult and her family warmly welcomed us. Those were happy days for all of us.

In the spring of 1927, the Jacobson family organized a reunion in Colona. Everyone was present except my sister-in-law Dorothy, who was eagerly awaiting the arrival of Margaret.

We spent almost another year in Wahoo while we awaited the Board's decision. However, unable to wait any longer, Ralph accepted a call to Bethesda, Iowa, where we spent the winter. As the prospects of returning to the Sudan gradually faded, Ralph developed an interest in Home Mission work. This led us to Verona, Missouri, where he served a small Augustana congregation.

After nearly a year in Verona, Synod finally decided to abstain from any work in the Sudan and instead focused all African efforts on Tanganyika. Naturally, Ralph felt disappointed by this outcome as he had hoped our church would also engage in Sudanese missions. At that time, we already had five children, and although I expressed interest in joining the Gunderson Mission, Ralph couldn't envision us embarking on such a venture with five young children. Consequently, we remained in Missouri.

MAMITA'S GRANDPARENTS VISIT IN VERONA (1929)

GRANDPA AND GRANDMA COME TO OUR HOUSE

Another big event filed in my memory bank was the visit of Mother's parents, Grandpa and Grandma Jacobson. Traveling by auto from their home 400 miles away in Illinois had to have been a formidable adventure in 1929.

Up until then their longest motor safari had been 200 miles to St. Louis to see their son play major league baseball. They arrived late and drove past Sportsman's Park just as a baseball flew over the wall in front of their car. When they got into their seats they discovered that the ball which nearly hit their car had been a home run hit by their own son.

Mother was beside herself with excitement as they drove up our driveway. I can clearly remember the happy sound of Grandma's hearty laugh as she hugged each of us. I can even recall clearly the nice odor of the leather upholstery of their big old touring car.

Grandpa stood tall and straight in spite of his seventy some years. We grandchildren were intrigued by his mustache which tickled when he nuzzled us. He had been quite an athlete and taught his son Bill most of the skills which started him on a career as a star major league baseball player. By the second day of his visit to Verona he became restless and looked for something to do. Our lawn had been mowed but there was tall grass around the edge. Grandpa found an old-fashioned scythe in the garage and efficiently cleaned up the rough edges around our house. He warned us to stay clear but we were close enough to enjoy watching him smoothly and rhythmically decapitating the weeds. Grandma pitched in, too, helping Mother with the household chores as they carried on a lively conversation.

Mamita

The most special treat of all came at our bedtime. Grandpa got out his fiddle and played us to sleep. His repertoire included lively versions of "Listen to the Mockingbird," "The Arkansas Traveler," and "The Irish Washerwoman." Grandpa had come from Sweden on a sailing vessel when he was seven years old. He remembered the sailors teasing him because he wore leather pants. When he was in his early teens he began working in the coal mines in Illinois. He continued until he had saved enough money to get married and finance a farm of his own. Somewhere along the line he bought a violin and taught himself to play. Before long he became much in demand to provide music for Saturday night dances. When my mother was in her teens she learned to accompany him on the piano. On another night at our house Grandpa took out his accordion and serenaded us at bedtime.

At that time I was nearing my fifth birthday and Paul had introduced me to the world of numbers. I had taught myself to write them from the page numerals in a book and was filling a notebook with them in consecutive order. Grandpa was sitting nearby reading the paper when I reached an obstacle. I looked up and asked him, "Grandpa, what comes after nine hundred and ninety nine?" He glanced at me with astonishment and burst out laughing. My first reaction was that he thought his grandkid was pretty dumb, but I was reassured when he told Grandma, "John has written his numbers up to one thousand and he hasn't even started to school!"

The end of their visit came all too soon. We were saddened as they loaded up and drove away. We didn't see them again until their Golden Wedding celebration in Illinois eight years later.

John E. Hult, Growing Up in the Ozarks. (Bolivar MO: Quiet Waters Publications 2001).

Mamita

A couple of small Augustana congregations were located east of Springfield, in former Swedish settlements beside Verona, west of Springfield. This sparked Ralph's interest in obtaining a home in or near Springfield, as he believed he could minister to all of them from there. Thus, he purchased what is now known as the Homestead. For months, he would drive to Verona every Sunday while also serving the other two congregations and providing ministry to some Augustana individuals in Springfield.

Around that time, there was a movement to close all the little churches of our Synod in that area. Despite various official visits, this eventually came to pass. As a result, we found ourselves in Springfield, with Ralph being dropped by both the Foreign and Home Mission Boards. It was also the era of the Great Depression, and there was no choice but to remain where we were.

Those were challenging years, as you older children surely remember, and you experienced the difficulties alongside us. However, despite the hardships, we had a joyful home and learned to appreciate life's simple pleasures. We all cherished our little farm, even though it was difficult to make progress with limited resources. The most challenging part was keeping up with the payments on our home. Ralph was on the

144

verge of losing his Pension and Aid because he couldn't meet the payments. Fortunately, fellow pastors in Nebraska came to our aid. I have been immensely grateful for that pension since Ralph's passing, and even to this day, it has greatly supported our family's education.

By 1938, when Paul turned 16 and became eligible for a driver's license, Ralph believed he could take on temporary pastoral assignments. He spent one summer in North Dakota, and although we could have relocated there, Ralph couldn't envision it. Subsequently, he received assignments in Osceola, Nebraska, and later in Rapid River, Michigan. After spending the winter there, the plan was for the family to join him during the summer in Stonington. It turned out to be a truly wonderful summer spent together.

Mutti

Leipzig (1928-1939)

We briefly lived near the city center, but in April 1928, we moved into a lovely newly built apartment in the southern part of Leipzig, on Windscheidstraße, just five minutes away from Muttel's apartment. After a year, our youngest, Klaus, was born on May 6, 1929.

On January 25, 1935, my beloved mother, Muttel, passed away at the St. Elisabeth Hospital in Leipzig-Connewitz.

On June 22, 1935, grandparents Moritz and Clara Trobisch celebrated their Golden Wedding anniversary with their four children, sons-in-law, daughters-in-law, and three grandchildren. They were caring grandparents to our children. Grandfather Moritz Trobisch passed away in December 1938. On the third day of Christmas in 1939, Grandmother Klara Trobisch closed her eyes forever.

The children had a harmonious childhood. All three attended secondary school after primary school and completed their high school education with the Abitur.

The reign of National Socialism only tangentially touched our family life. Martin steadfastly resisted

146

becoming a member of the Nazi Party, and Walter and Hertha led groups for the deaf youth at the Leipzig School for the Deaf, which allowed them to avoid the disadvantages of the Hitler Youth.

The Second World War soon began to destroy our harmonious family life and tear our family apart. Walter was a student in the final year of the Petrischule (Realgymnasium). Many of his classmates took emergency exams and immediately joined the military. However, for Walter, passing his final exams according to regulations was more important than being a soldier. He still had enough time for both.

LEIPZIG WINDSCHEIDSTRASSE (1928)

We briefly lived near the city center, but in April 1928, we moved into a lovely newly built apartment in the southern part of Leipzig, on Windscheidstraße, just five minutes away from Muttel's apartment. After a year, our youngest, Klaus, was born on May 6, 1929.

Historic Residential Complex on Gustav-Freytag-Strasse 19-23 at the corner of Windscheidstraße

Description:

Built between 1925-1926, the residential complex on Gustav-Freytag-Strasse 19-23, designed by Fritz Riemann for the Non-Profit Civil Servants' Building Association, remains an architectural gem with historical significance. The three-winged complex, featuring an Art Deco stucco facade, boasts a front garden enclosed by a charming low artificial stone wall.

Distinctive features:

- Central Building: Rising four stories high, the central building stands proudly at the corner of Windscheidstraße. Its two entrances facing Gustav-Freytag-Strasse are adorned with a broad cross-gable over the pedestrian eave. Polygonal corner cores, along with staircases and corner turrets projecting forward, add a touch of elegance.

- Side Wings: Embracing a serene courtyard, the three-story side wings feature a developed mansard floor, creating a harmonious ensemble. The complex showcases a grouped structure with height gradation towards the center, complemented by an animated roof landscape.

- Architectural Details: Horizontal grouping through a narrow string course enhances the facade's appeal. Art Deco style architectural decorations adorn entrances and bay windows, while ground floor windows boast arch blinds, lending a timeless charm to the building.

- Artistic Elements: Notably, two life-sized cast stone female figures grace the mansard floor facing Windscheidstraße, adding an artistic touch to the architectural design. Loggias on the courtyard side provide a relaxing retreat for the residents.

Originally comprising 33 smaller three or four-room apartments, the complex featured a front garden and a protective fence, enhancing its residential charm. Over the years, this historic gem has retained its architectural allure, capturing the essence of its era while standing as a testament to the city's heritage.

Translated from: Wikipedia (German) Liste der Kulturdenkmale in Connewitz

WORLD WAR II (1940-1945)

Mamita

Zamzam (1940-1941)

In the winter of 1940, the Mission Board again called Ralph to go to Africa and serve during the war. Just as before, the German missionaries had to leave their stations. Although one Board member had previously told Ralph that the time would come when they would ask him to serve in Africa again, it felt like a remarkable turn of events. And so it happened. Ralph returned to Springfield in January 1941, and in March, he boarded the ill-fated Zamzam, which was sunk by a German raider. The book "Zamzam" provides a detailed account of this experience.

It wasn't until June 1941 that Ralph finally returned. David, Paul, and I went to Colona to meet him, filled with anticipation and joy at his safe homecoming.

Of course, we were overjoyed to have Daddy back with us. But from then on, the Board was determined to find another way to send him to Africa. Meanwhile, America was at war with Japan and Germany, adding to the situation's complexities.

During that fall and winter, Ralph was frequently away from home, giving speeches and preparing for Africa. His suitcases remained packed for weeks and months, ready for his journey.

SINKING OF THE ZAM ZAM (RALPH HULT, 1941)

Ralph returned to Springfield in January 1941, and in March, he boarded the ill-fated Zamzam, which was sunk by a German raider. The book "Zamzam" provides a detailed account of this experience. (Mamita's Manuscript)

"Passing Through the Waters"

By Rev. Ralph D. Hult

"But now, thus saith the Lord ... : Fear not, for I have redeemed thee; I have called thee by thy name, thou art mine. When thou passeth through the waters, I will be with thee. . .. Fear not; for I am with thee. Thus saith the Lord, who maketh a way in the sea, and a path in the mighty waters." - Isaiah 43.

In the early morning of April 17, I was suddenly awakened by a "bang." It seemed as though a huge wave had slapped the ship and dashed over the deck. What could it be? I could not look out as the glass in the porthole of our cabin had been painted. The sea seemed to be calm. No, it could not be a wave. With such thoughts flashing through my mind, I arose.

"Wham-Bang!"

Overhead and toward the front of the ship, I heard things crashing and falling. Now it dawned on me what all the confusion was about. Our ship was being shelled.

One of my two cabin mates had risen very early that morning. He came rushing in, and we asked him what was happening. His answer was, "A raider!" A moment later, we heard another "Wham-Bang."

Now the light in our cabin became quite dim, and for a few moments, it seemed as though we were doomed to go down in darkness. There was no time to lose. The other cabin mate and I dressed hurriedly. As we stepped out of the cabin, we saw two of our neighbors lying helpless at the foot of the nearby stairway. We paused to see if we could help and found that the two wounded men were being cared for by their companions. The long, narrow corridor was full of frightened passengers trying to get out, but there was no panic. As we were slowly working our way out of the place, we were relieved to observe that the shelling had ceased.

When we finally reached the open space on our deck, near the rear hatch, we could distinguish the dark form of a ship in the distance. Signal lights were flashing from it. Our lifeboat station was on the deck above, so we had to climb a narrow and steep outside stairway. Many were trying to get up this stairway, so we made very slow progress, but at last we reached the upper deck.

As we approached our station, we saw the Egyptians lowering the boat from the boat deck above. When it reached the level of our deck, the women and children were helped into it, among them Mrs. Danielson and her children. Two of the boats on our side of the ship had been destroyed by the shelling, so there was considerable crowding at our station. When the boat had been filled to its capacity, the sailors shouted, "No more, no more!" And we were lowered to the water.

As soon as the ropes that held our boat were unloosed, we noticed that it was taking water. The seamen were asked to refasten the ropes, but they insisted that we would be able to bail out the water. The oars were worked, and we moved toward the stern of the sinking Zamzam.

In a few minutes, we were up to our knees in water, and it was evident that our boat had been very badly damaged. It was impossible to bail out the water fast enough. In the excitement, there was some shifting of positions in the boat, and suddenly it turned over! How thankful we were to the Ruler of wind and wave that the sea was calm!

As the boat turned over, some of its occupants were thrown some distance. As I was one of the last to enter the boat, I was near the rudder and so just slipped into the water. At no time did I go under.

I do not swim, and so I was very grateful for the support of my life preserver and an oar which floated within my reach. I soon managed to get near enough to the overturned boat to grasp one of the rope loops on its side.

As soon as I felt myself anchored in this way to the boat, I thought of Mrs. Danielson and her children. What a relief it was to see them nearby, all still afloat! But how long could they stay above water?

As I saw that brave mother with her youngest gripped in the crook of her left arm, my soul cried out to Almighty God for help. And I also pleaded with the Egyptian seamen, who had managed to crawl up on the overturned boat, and now sat there with uplifted arms calling on Allah, to lower their hands and try to reach the children and draw them out of the water. They did succeed in reaching some of the children, thank God!

"What next?" was the question in our minds, as we managed to close in around our overturned lifeboat. How long could we hold out, floating about in the ocean?

As we looked in the direction of the raider, we observed that it was slowly moving toward us. It also seemed as though we were drifting toward the approaching warship. After a while, we found ourselves right at its side, and were in danger of being caught in its propellers.

Thank God, the German sailors were trying to reach us with ropes. After several efforts, we managed to hold fast to their ropes and as soon as the raider's lifeboats could be lowered, they came to our rescue. How wonderful it seemed to feel strong arms draw us out of the water!

Thank God, our feet had found a footing again!

The small children were lifted up to the ship's deck in a rope basket. The older children and the grownups climbed up on a rope ladder. The occupants of our boat were the first to reach the raider's deck.

As we stood there watching our fellow passengers and the crew members one after the other arriving on the deck, our hearts sang praises to God for His deliverance. Surely, He had been very near, "a very present help," as we passed through the waters that morning. Had He not intervened on our behalf? The very hands that but a little while ago were wielding those terrible instruments of destruction were now efficiently ministering to our needs.

"With courage, strength, and hope renewed" we beheld His glorious sun rising in the direction of the great Dark Continent. In the western sky, we beheld a glorious bow, arching the sky.

Ralph Hult, "Passing Through Waters" 46-49. In: S. Hjalmar Swanson (editor), ZAMZAM: The Story of a Strange Missionary Odyssey (Quiet Waters Publications, Bolivar 2007). Reprint of the Fifth Printing, January 1944 of the 1941 edition published by the Board of Foreign Missions of the Augustana Synod.

Mamita

Ralph Leaving for Africa Again (1942)

By May 1st, 1942, Ralph had found a ship on which he could travel.

Ingrid had already spent two years at Luther Academy in Wahoo, living with Grandma Hult. I wished Paul and John could join her, but it seemed impossible. When Ingrid was ready for high school, we faced the same difficulties. I wrote to Grandma about it, and she graciously offered to provide room and board for Ingrid. And so, she was able to attend. Then, when Ralph was home after the Zamzam, we enrolled Veda and Ingrid at the local high school in Rogersville alongside John. Paul had already graduated from there and had spent a year at the University of Missouri. The following year (1942-1943), the three girls could attend Luther Academy in Wahoo. John would have loved to go too, but I needed him at home then. Paul had been working in Moline and knew he would soon be drafted, so he chose to enlist in the Marines. The war cast a dark shadow over us, and we knew it wouldn't be long before John would also have to go.

One day, as I contemplated all these things—the war, Ralph leaving, and the boys' departure—I told Ralph, "How I wish I could move to Wahoo or Lindsborg while you are away for the sake of the children." This remark angered him deeply. Although he never became physically aggressive when angry, he typically channeled his emotions into hard work. He responded with silence, barely speaking, but worked feverishly throughout the day and seemed greatly hurt. It pained him to think that I had even considered leaving our beloved little home, which he believed was the best place for our family. In response, I made a promise never to mention leaving again.

After Ralph's passing in Dar-es-Salaam, Tanganyika, on March 18, 1943, we did move to Wahoo. The war was still ongoing. Looking back, I genuinely believe that those four years we spent in Wahoo were where God intended us to be.

RALPH HULT'S LAST LETTER TO MAMITA (MARCH 4-6, 1943)

Dar-es-Salaam, March fourth, 1943. Dear Gertrude, Oh! -- if instead of sitting down to my "Corona," I might sit down beside my beloved for a little visit, or better still go with her for a walk out to the seaside! – As that cannot be, I shall have to be satisfied with the former alternative.

I must confess that it is with a degree of hesitation that I sit down to write these lines which are to accompany a little gift to the woman I love.

Gertrude, dear, since coming to Africa this time without you and without the prospect of having you join me in the near future (as was the case the first time I came without you) -- I have come to realize, as never before, how much you have meant to me for the past twenty-five years and more, -- how much you mean to me --

Mamita

NOW, -- how much I NEED you now. In recent months as I have had to live in memories so many, [many] things have come to my mind which have caused me much heart-searching.

I have been thinking particularly of recent years, years in which my work has taken me away from HOME and loved ones, -- years in which my beloved has had to bear more than her share of family responsibilities. --"Has it been right for me to accept work that has involved our separation for such long periods????" -- This question, of course, disturbs me at this time, a time when you perhaps need me (and I need YOU) more than ever. -- This is a trying time for both of us as individuals even under normal circumstances. -- This, and similar questions have simply bombarded me in recent months.

Under such circumstances, I have sought comfort in our common faith. I can say this much that PRAYER for loved ones, specific prayer, has meant more to me than ever before in my life. In moments of Prayer, I have seemed close to you. -- And still, I have longed intensely for your physical presence, making it possible for us to consider together problems of the present and future, as well as to try to understand our past experiences. I feel that this is very, very important at this time in our lives. Even at this rather late stage we begin to make a real effort to understand ourselves.

I have done much thinking (in these lonely days) along certain lines, as I have sought to understand myself. There are so many, many things in life that puzzle one. My mind has wandered back to experiences of early and late childhood. -- These days followed by those days of early Adolescence (What days they were for me !! out there on the prairies of Nebraska). What conflicts! -- What agonizing days they were! - OH - if at that time I could have known some of the things I know now and which every boy and girl of that age should know -- How different my life might have been. -- But I thank God for His grace, sufficient to carry me through those difficult years, more difficult than need have been.

-- How I longed, how I yearned those days to LOVE and to BE LOVED. - How I longed to meet someone who I could believe had faith in me, someone with whom I could share every HOPE and AMBITION, - someone who could and would understand me.

Friday, March 5th, 8:30 P.M. -- Well, here we are again. -- Have just come up to my room from my evening meal. Remained at the table rather long. Reason was that I got into a very interesting conversation with my table mate, a man who has recently come down here from a neighboring colony. In the near future, he expects to have his wife and little son with him. She is a South African. -- How nice it would be if the writer of these lines could look forward to the early arrival of his wife and family -- Well, it's pleasant to "rejoice with those who rejoice."

I was happily surprised this morning to find a letter in my box from Cloquet, Minnesota postmarked November 10th. It was meant to be a Christmas greeting. Although it didn't reach me for Christmas, it certainly was nice to get it at this time. Ida writes, "It feels so good to know that you are in Africa again. If only we were there too. But there is work to be done here at home, too, while we wait." -- Further on, she writes, "America is becoming world-minded. She is becoming conscious of all peoples and races. God willing we live to see the end of this war, we should see a mighty Foreign Missions era. May we prepare ourselves to meet it." --- It did me so much good to read Ida's letter. Quite in line with the thought of yesterday evening. I was happily surprised also to receive Christmas Greetings from the Wyman sisters. Ellen writes, "We rejoice with you that you are now in the land of your heart's desire and that you now have the privilege of sharing God's Word with our black brothers and sisters. May the Lord use you mightily in His service." Of course, I appreciate hearing from these our friends. Ellen mentioned having managed to get my films and expressed the hope that I may have received prints from them. I can't tell you how much I appreciate the prints you sent me. They mean so much to me. I have shown them to a good many and they all seem so interested in them.

This morning, as I was reading my Bible, I heard a "Hodi" at the door. I was a bit surprised to have a caller so early (it was before seven o'clock). I didn't go to the door but called out "Kariboo" -- To my surprise, Mr. Jagsi walked in with a smile on his face. I invited him to sit down and offered to read to him the passage I was studying. He listened intently. Then I told him about the letter I had received from home yesterday evening and also showed him the snapshots. He seemed very interested in them, particularly the ones of Mother Hult and Father and Mother Jacobson. He has seen our family picture before. Then when there was a lull in the conversation, he said, "Now I have some news for you. You have ten children, now I have also." Their home has been blessed with a tenth child. He seemed so very happy to tell me all about the little boy that came to their home a day or two ago. Mr.Jagsi is employed in one of the banks of the city and has been on sick leave for some time, and now he has been able to return to his work. After this brief visit, he bade me "Goodbye" and left the room. A little while later, I was surprised to hear his voice outside the door again. In he walked with two parcels in his hands. He brought me some Indian delicacies. How I wish that I could send them home to you. I'm sure that you would enjoy them more than I possibly can. But I do appreciate his kindness.

That's how my day began. I've been very, very busy all day and so feel very tired this evening. Have just heard the newscast for the evening. Sounds encouraging. I suppose that you listen in every evening for the final summaries, or perhaps you are just too tired by that time. As last night, I shall go out for a little walk before retiring, planning to meet you again tomorrow for a conclusion of our visit. Nite-Nite.

Mamita

Saturday, March 6th, 11:00 A.M. -- Now I shall take time for a brief visit before noon, and then get these sheets over to the Post Office so that they may be on their way HOME-ward. There are so many, many things I might write about in this letter, but I shall promise you that I shall continue as soon as possible. I did plan to tell you something about my journey up-country, but that must wait. One thing, however, which I'm sure will interest David, Gustav, and Carl (and perhaps even his big brothers, and possibly even his sisters) -- I have now seen LIONS for the first time after all these years and all the safaris I have gone on in Africa. I saw three of them one evening. I HEARD them almost every evening, up in that country, especially when I was traveling, and, happily, a distance from the grass huts I was in. I won't write about that yet, but promise you more later. It's very interesting indeed. I also feel that it was worthwhile. I am looking forward to making another visit there.

I did plan to include a letter to PAUL in this. I was happy and relieved to hear that he is still in America for further training. That seems so very essential today when our boys have to face an enemy who has been training for decades, in fact, for generations. I was so happy to hear that Paul could speak to his MOTHER on her Birthday. Do you remember celebrating Paul's birthday two years ago? How nice it would have been if he could have been on our trip that evening.

I'm enclosing a little card for Paul and one for John. Please forward them with the next letter to the boys. I imagine we shall all be thinking of Paul on his birthday, a week in advance. I may send him a cable for his birthday. It's hardly possible that our "baby" is already twenty-one. God bless him and keep him.

Gertrude, before I bring this letter to close, I feel that I must write another word or two about my "loneliness". I'm sorry that it has come out in my letters more strongly than I wished, especially if it hurts and worries you. You'll understand that it's quite natural

162

to feel a bit lonely under the special circumstances that have prevailed since I left home. First, rather disappointing experiences on arriving, and I questioned for a time whether I was needed or wanted. In the midst of that depression came the news of your sever illness, which didn't help me, as I questioned whether I should have left for Africa at this time. Then, these many months of uncertainty and concern about the situation at home, the service, finances, etc., etc. Add to that the initial difficulties of adjustment to the work in whatever position and the difficulty of the language. And, I'm nearing the fifty-fifth year of my life. There's hardly any comparison with the situation of 1919 when I left my bride of a few months. God hadn't made it easy for us (nor for her), but after all, it was different with my wife, now the MOTHER of ten --- and this under WAR conditions. Please remember this, Gertrude, as an explanation of my loneliness.

God is good. He is supplying strength for body and mind from day to day. The arrival of the messages from Dr. Stone one after the other is also helping me very much. Now I know the circumstances at home better and so can think more clearly, more definitely. That makes a world difference.

God bless and keep you, one and all, with Love,

> *Typoscript. A line written by hand at the top of the page says, "Copy of letter sent by surface mail."*

MAMITA RECEIVES THE NEWS OF RALPH HULT'S DEATH (MARCH 18, 1943)

After Ralph's passing in Dar-es-Salaam, Tanganyika, on March 18, 1943, we did move to Wahoo. The war was still ongoing. (Mamita's Manuscript)

Then we received news of Father's assignment. He had been appointed superintendent of the Usaramo District, a territory so large it was formerly served by at least a score of missionaries. Now Father would have to handle it alone.

He was to be stationed at Dar es Salaam, the capital of Tanzania and one of its main ports. Dar was considered a "hardship post," for the climate was steaming, and at that time disease was rampant. Father did not mind, so great was his happiness at being once more in the work.

"I have arrived at Dar at the beginning of the hot season," he wrote us. "You can imagine how I perspire in this sticky heat. … I try to get enough sleep, though it is difficult in the heat of the night—and one never wakens refreshed. I walk to the waterfront early in the morning and again in the evening. It is so refreshing to get even slight breezes from off the water. … At times I am almost sick with my longing to see you and be with you. … It is now five months since the last letter I received from you was written—July 23."

It made our hearts ache, for we had faithfully answered each one of his, telling him about our activities, of the fine year we were having at the Academy. We had enclosed snapshots of us and clippings from the school paper.

We were looking forward to the Spring Youth Conference to be held in March. One of our speakers was to be a missionary from Africa, Mrs. George Anderson, and we knew Father would enjoy hearing about that. Young people were to join us from all parts of Nebraska.

Our Youth Conference was everything we expected. There was a feeling of spring in the air the following Monday morning. The last traces of snow were melting away, I was resting between classes in my room. In a few minutes the bell would ring for our ten o'clock period. Suddenly, I heard a knock on the door.

"Come in," I called out without bothering to get up. I was startled to see Pastor Lauersen, our new president, standing in the doorway. I was even more alarmed when I saw that Veda and Eunie were with him. Why should he be here in the Girls' Dorm? What was wrong?

In a flash I thought of that other Monday morning, just two years ago, when Dr. Lindberg had stopped me on the stairs of Old Main and called me into his office. Then it was to tell me the news of the sinking of the *Zamzam*. What would it be this time? I felt it even before he told us.

President Lauersen was solemn.

"I wanted you girls to be all together before I say what I have to say," he declared.

We exchanged glances.

"A cablegram has just been received from Dar es Salaam. Your father passed away from heart failure following malaria on March 18."

He had broken it to us as gently as he could.

That other time I had said to myself: "I know my father's not dead. He's alive. I'll see him again."

But this time I knew with a great finality that my father was dead.

This was the greatest blow of my life.

165

Mamita

I think I might have fainted had I not felt that countless arms of love were upholding me. I was aware of the reservoirs of a new strength—something that I had never before experienced. Veda and Eunie wept almost hysterically at the first shock of the news. But as we fell into each other's arms, we knew a great comfort, a comfort from outside ourselves.

Pastor Lauersen continued: "Your mother, down in Springfield alone with your five youngest brothers and sisters, has not heard. You're the one who must tell her, Ingrid. Your uncle is here, waiting to take you to your grandmother's home. She will need you, too. You will also need her this day," he said.

We found our grandmother with tears in her eyes, yet her face was serene. My uncle had already told her of the cablegram.

"It's no surprise to me," she said. "Strange, but for these last days I have known in my heart that Ralph was no longer on this earth." She looked up then at his picture. It was hanging above a photograph of her husband, who also had died unexpectedly when he was in his early fifties. "It makes me long all the more to be with them in heaven," she said with a sigh. Tomorrow would be her seventy-ninth birthday.

From my grandmother's house I called Mother at the Homestead. She answered the phone and greeted me with her usual cheeriness.

"Mother," I said, "I have some bad news for you."

"Yes, Ingrid, tell me what it is," she said slowly.

I read her the cablegram we had received from the mission office. There was a long moment of silence. Then she asked me in a normal voice how we were; she was especially concerned about Grandmother.

Mamita

I learned later what a hard day it had been for her. Carl was sick with the measles, and the other children were coming down with them. Also, she had two hundred baby chicks to care for. She simply had no time to give herself over to grief, and as she wrote us, perhaps this was her greatest help in enduring the shock of the news.

When she came to Wahoo for the memorial service for Father, I tried to think of some way to comfort her. She answered me simply: "You do not yet realize, Ingrid, what it means to lose your life partner."

Ingrid Trobisch, On Our Way Rejoicing (Quiet Waters Publications: Springfield, Missouri, 2000).

BIOGRAPHICAL DATES - RALPH DANIEL HULT

Education:

Luther College, Wahoo, NE: 1906-1910

Augustana College, Rock Island, IL: 1910-1913

Graduated, 1913

English Lutheran Seminary, Maywood, IL: 1914-1916

Augustana Seminary: 1916-1917; Ordained 1917 on a call to establish a mission in the Sudan, Africa.

Kennedy School of Missions, Hartford, CT: 1917-1919

Service:

Missionary to Mormons in Utah: 1914

Sudan, Africa: 1919-1922

Mamita

Tanganyika, Africa: 1922-1926

Home Missions: Missouri, Nebraska, N. Dakota, Iowa and Michigan: 1926-1941

On the Zamzam enroute to Africa when it was shelled: 1941

Tanganyika, Africa: 1942-1943

Died March 18, 1943, in Dar es Salaam, Tanganyika

> *Quoted from a typoscript: Two Years in the Life of Ralph Hult.*
> *Excerpts from diaries, 1917 and 1919. Edited by Adeline Hult.*
> *1991.*

Mutti

War Years (1942-1945)

At Easter 1942, Walter passed his Abitur [high school diploma], and a few days later, on March 23, 1942, he was drafted into the military. He was sent to a training camp for officer candidates in Neustadt an der Mettau, in the formerly "reclaimed" Czechoslovakia. I could even visit him once when he had to spend a few weeks in the infirmary there. Then he had to go to the front, specifically to Russia, as the Second World War had been raging for over two years.

Walter was wounded three times. After his second injury in southern Russia - a gunshot fracture in his left upper arm - he was admitted to a hospital in Vienna on September 21, 1943. With the help of a Catholic chief physician, he was permitted to enroll in the theological faculty. He studied in Vienna for two semesters. Then he had to return to the field, to Italy, where he was wounded again.

Hertha completed her Abitur in 1943 and immediately joined the labor service (RAD) in Luisenhof near Stargard in Pomerania. She did not go willingly. Her last entry in her diary on April 5, 1943, reads: "I want to preserve the good within me and stay pure."

However, friendships with other young women and the understanding of the camp leader, a woman, eventually made her appreciate her stay. After six months, she did not have to go to Berlin for war auxiliary service like almost everyone else but remained in the camp as the senior comrade. Shortly after Christmas 1943, she returned on leave to Leipzig, then returned to the camp on January 17, 1944, and fell ill with diphtheria. After only four days of illness, she passed away on January 25, 1944, at Stargard Hospital. With the help of the camp leader, we obtained permission, despite the chaos of war, alarms, and poor transportation conditions, to have the sealed coffin transferred, allowing us to bury our only daughter in Leipzig's Südfriedhof. We laid her to rest in the grave that was originally intended for us.

Klaus, attending secondary school then, had to visit several youth training camps but narrowly avoided military service. He was able to finish school and help me repair our apartment, which the bombs had heavily damaged.

Martin had been evacuated with his class in January 1944 and spent a frigid and snowy winter in the Erzgebirge. He had obtained a specialized teaching qualification in shorthand, and shortly before the war, he had also successfully passed the examination for teaching typewriting. That's why in May 1944, he was suddenly called back to Leipzig and reassigned as a specialized teacher at a vocational school. Unfortunately, fate had it that in April, before this happened, I had heeded his urgent pleas to leave the bomb-threatened Leipzig and joined him with Klaus in the Erzgebirge. So, when Martin moved back to Leipzig, I stayed, rented a place, and Klaus attended secondary school, the Oberschule in Obernhau.

We were reunited once again during the summer vacation on the crest of the Erzgebirge, and then we all returned to Leipzig.

Walter experienced the end of the war in southern Germany, was captured by an African American soldier in Kairlindach (by the way, the first Black person he had ever seen in his life), and was interned in the Langenzenn prisoner-of-war camp near Nuremberg. From there, he walked home as our troops had destroyed railways and bridges. He arrived safely on May 25, 1945.

Martin's brother and my brother-in-law, Hans Trobisch, returned safely from World War II. However, as he had been an Ortsgruppenleiter under Hitler, he was reported, arrested, and sent to a Russian camp, from which he never returned.

LETTERS FROM THE EASTERN FRONT (STALINGRAD 1942/43)

Then he [Walter] had to go to the front, specifically to Russia,
as the Second World War had been raging for over two years.
(Mutti)

[Editorial note from Caffier/Stephen Trobisch: On November 22, a sig-
nificant Russian offensive was launched. The German troops at Stalin-
grad near Kalach-on-Don were cut off from the units in the hinterland,
effectively encircling the Germans at Stalingrad.]

December 9, 1942 *

Dear Loved Ones,

Thank you so much for your enriching letter! I had anticipated
that you might not fully comprehend the account of our conditions here.

Comment: I can't provide detailed descriptions of our locations.
You'll have to create your own mental picture. Fortunately, our
steel helmets are stored on the lockers; otherwise, the lack of space
would be even worse. We call our beds 'ladders' due to the cross-
boards that support the straw-filled sacks; they indeed look and
often feel like ladders from the top and the bottom.

As for the "girls" it's part of our "room decorations." We aim to
cover the walls as much as possible. The portraits of our leaders
and Knights Cross holders are placed alongside those of film di-
vas, bathing girls, scantily dressed, and even nude women. Thus,
a mix of various images hangs on our walls. For instance, Rom-
mel, bent over maps, is situated above an image of such a girl, and
so on.

172

Mutti

Rumor has it that the 4/465 unit is meant to move to Warsaw. I hope that this move doesn't compromise our entire vacation. But it's happening now.

Warmest regards, Walter

December 14, 1942

Dear Ones,

Nothing pains me more than the thought of burdening you with fears and worries during Christmas. Thus, this letter is meant to bring you joy: I am well and healthy. You should know that this letter may sound different from my earlier ones. It's written by someone who has now seen the full misery of war with his own eyes. I haven't been spared much, from the physical and mental strain to the torment of death and violence. Yet, incredibly, I have been safeguarded from it all, even when death came close.

On December 3, we were deployed about 200 kilometers from the great city [a required euphemism for Stalingrad], which has been bitterly contested for so long. Deployment was preceded by endless marches, day and night. That morning, I experienced my baptism by fire. We suffered numerous casualties, which I don't wish to elaborate on. We had to dig into the frozen winter soil and spend the night in these dirt holes, exposed to enemy fire. For the following ten days, we lived under the open sky, moving up or back to different hills in response to the changing front. There were days when we had to bury ourselves in the ground up to our necks, expecting tanks to rage over us at any moment. We were encircled without supplies for two days, fearing enemy assaults from behind. Living in dirt holes, the lack of sleep, continuous anxiety, the cold and especially the wet took a toll on us. It's astounding what a human being can endure! I never thought one could wear completely soaked fur boots for so long without falling ill. Now, however, my toes have frozen, which is why I'm staying behind at the supplies. Although I'm still in danger, I can at least stay in a closed room with a stove.

Recent experiences have broadened my perspective on many things in life, causing me to change many of my opinions. Currently, our company is stationed securely on a hill in a straw barn. The battle has increasingly turned into a tank battle. During good weather, Stukas are also extensively used. We, the infantry, bide our time.

This Advent season is a memorable one. Christmas isn't going to be very festive. Despite everything, I hope to escape this misery soon. I have a vague feeling that maybe we will be relieved.

Since receiving your airmail letter on November 21, I haven't heard further from you. But I hope that mail will be sent to us soon. For now, I can only write to you. Please share this information with everyone who inquires about me. It's impossible for me to write to everyone. My only wish is for this letter to reach you soon, although that's quite uncertain.

Loving greetings, Your Walter

Christmas 1942

[Walter wrote in his journal: "I cannot let myself die because I have not yet mailed the Christmas present for my mother." He attached ten poems to the following letter.]

Dear Mutti,

"Just as a mother comforts her child, so will I comfort you," says the Lord. Could He offer a greater promise? At the same time, could anything grander be said of a mother?

As He comforts us in the way a mother would, He also comforts us through our mothers. Similarly, I didn't write these poems alone; you were a part of their creation. If I gift them to you, I'm merely returning what's yours, a humble echo of your love. Still, I'm grateful that I'm capable of producing this echo.

These words belong to you alone, and no one else shall see them unless you wish it so. You're the only one who can truly understand them. Therefore, I don't need to explain the extent of my suffering.

It's not merely the hardships I've endured or the misery I've witnessed that pains me; it's the loneliness, the torment amplified by the bleak surroundings. Amidst utter incomprehension, on endless marches, and on the brink of physical exhaustion, I found the words. Often, I would spend an entire day searching for a single syllable. Yet, when I would collapse, exhausted at a makeshift campsite, I felt that instead of mindlessly contributing to destruction, I had created something meaningful.

I carried this little work with me as if it were a sacred relic, a testament to your love, a beacon of life amidst death and horror. Later, I could barely decipher the characters I had scrawled with hands stiff from cold. But was it necessary? I had the words engraved in my heart.

In my heart, a peculiar sense of security was born that persisted even when others were no longer there. Whenever I remembered those tiny slips of paper in my packet, I knew: this cannot be the end; my task is not finished. I haven't sent them off yet. I had a certainty that I would soon have the opportunity to complete everything. And this is precisely what happened.

The poems touch on life's end. Thus, we should discuss the end candidly.

I know these will be of great value to you if I were to die. Their message is twofold: Firstly, nothing surpasses my longing for a homecoming in the Kingdom of Love. Secondly, if I remain on this earth, I feel redeemed, freed from the Kingdom of Death.

175

Mutti

I thank God for comforting me as a mother would. I thank you, dearest Mother!

Your Walter

December 25, 1942

[This letter was received on January 6, 1943]

Dearest Ones! Dear Mutti!

Day of Rejoicing! Day of Rejoicing! Before you read this letter, please pray the Lord's Prayer with more gratitude than ever before. Your Walter has escaped hell. I am safe and secure.

I want to tell you straight away: I have been wounded. One should never wish harm upon oneself, but my wound is a Christmas gift from heaven.

On December 23, at dawn, I was shot by a Russian submachine gun. The bullet passed right through my right thigh. "Oh, this is a beautiful one," say the doctors each time they inspect my leg and smile. The bullet went through cleanly without injuring the bone. What a stroke of luck!

Currently, I lie in a field hospital, 60 kilometers to the rear. I'm waiting for transport, which is delayed due to the lack of a locomotive, though the hospital train is ready otherwise.

Just imagine: there's a chance I may be coming home. Then, you might be able to visit me. Just keep your fingers crossed!

Yesterday, for Christmas Eve, we had chocolate, cookies, candy, and tea with rum - and each one of us had a Stollen [Christmas cake]. Even a Christmas tree with candles is here, though it's only a larch.

My only sorrow was that you didn't know about my fortunate fate. Every minute, I was with you in spirit, knowing so well your

176

traditions of this day. This joyous letter should now literally fly to you.

For now, stop writing, since any mail will just end up being burned.

I've received your letters 1-5, 10, 15, 19, and 20. I cried unrestrainedly when I read them in my dirt hole. I couldn't help it. I was no longer accustomed to so much love. I have three packages, the first two, and the large one with the Bible, which I fortunately brought along. I had to leave other things behind. But what does it matter? I am saved.

I barely feel any pain anymore, at least it's quite bearable. My leg is in a splint. I just have to get used to lying down. The doctors say I should be able to walk again in four weeks.

Let the day this letter arrives be a special day for you by celebrating in some unique way. I might get home sooner than this letter.

Rejoice with me. I am so happy to be out of that pandemonium. Please greet everyone and spread the news! Here's to a happy New Year,

Your exhilarated Walter

January 5, 1943

Dear ones,

I just had a cup of black tea. It reminded me so much of mother that I finally decided to write a letter. I almost rejoiced too soon in my last letter, for I had a close shave with death once again. But from then until this cup of tea, it's a long story.

I will start from the point where we went forward again after warming up for a few days with the support units. In a way, I was glad about this, for we indeed felt less safe in the rear than on the front line. The whole village was constantly on alert against enemy tanks, which put everyone into great nervousness. This was all the more understandable, as this village had once been overrun by tanks. This must have been on the days when we were surrounded by the enemy. I wrote to you about it. The traces of this raid were still very clear to see. The Russians had captured all our schnapps and in their drunkenness had wrought the cruelest havoc. The wounded in the infirmary had been murdered in a horrible way. Many had fled to a ravine and were simply crushed there. They were transported away for days. Thank God that you have never had to look into a mass grave. On the street, you could literally not walk straight for human and horse corpses. Then there was the stench. I remember a year ago, I took a detour through Adolf Hitler Street on my way back from school because there had been a dead cat on Kaiser Wilhelm Street in the morning. How different things are now! But I can still cry. That reassured me deeply.

So on the one hand, I was quite glad to be able to escape from this horrible place. However, I dreaded the march (15 km) like never before. My feet had swelled up in the warmth. Added to this was a sort of rheumatism. Both my heels were open. At any rate, I walked like an old man. Fortunately, I was able to sit on a vehicle part of the way, otherwise I might not have made it.

The company had meanwhile moved to a different height. I immediately had to dig a machine gun position with one other person. It took all night. After three spade thrusts, we had to sit down. We were that tired and weak. I seriously considered plans to report sick. But the mail was just about to be delivered. I didn't want to miss it for a second time. So I decided to at least wait for my parcels. Then I would really be ready. To some extent, this worked.

There's one more incident I want to briefly recount: It was the night from December 20th to 21st. We were so far into our dig that we both could sit upright. So it was by no means tank-proof. We covered the head ends against cold and snow with tarpaulins. There was a gap in the middle where the machine gun stood. Behind us, about 20 meters away, was a German assault gun. To prevent it from freezing, it would occasionally run its engine. In addition, our own artillery constantly shot over us. Since we didn't have guard duty at that moment, we were dozing in semi-sleep and thus didn't react to the shooting or engine sound. But after a while, it all seemed too much for me. I crawled out from under my tarpaulin and saw a tank standing a few meters away, slightly to the right, with the barrel pointed backwards. At first, it wasn't clear to me that it was a Russian tank. I immediately woke my comrade, who had more experience. We clearly heard the Russians talking, pulled in the machine gun, and readied our pistols in case the guys climbed out. We looked helplessly towards our assault gun. It was still in its old place and silent. Why?

Now another Russian said something, probably: "Try to go backward." (He had already taken a hit and couldn't move forward.) Another anxious moment: Was he just backing up to run over us more easily? After he backed up about 30 meters, he was hit directly by the assault gun. Big detonation. It was clear to both of us: had he been shot in front of our hole, it would have torn us apart.

The attack was repelled. About eight tanks were burning on the hill in front of us. The following infantry, which was actually our primary task to combat, had fled. The situation soon became clear. The assault gun hadn't fired because its firing pin had broken at the critical moment.

[...]

Now, to my injury. It happened in a most peaceful manner, from A to Z, it's a stroke of luck. No fighting, noise or nerves. Listen: I wanted to make coffee (or rather herbal tea, the taste is so similar that we gradually call every drink "coffee"). The coffee we got in

179

the evening we drank immediately, as it would freeze within minutes. Therefore, there was great thirst in the morning. So, someone always had to melt snow on a fire and with much patience, make something drinkable. I had volunteered, mainly to sit by the fire.

Now, probably under the cover of night, a Russian had crept into one of the shot tanks. At dawn, I crawl out of my hole. It was utterly quiet. Frost lay on the steppe grass. I go to the next hole to wake someone to take over my guard duty. As I stood upright in front of his dwelling, it goes: "Pitsch". I feel a hard blow against my right thigh and immediately fall flat. Initially, of course, great shock and pain. Loud cries for help. Gradually, though, I realize that I can still stand and limp back to the medic's hole. The first fear was already over when I saw the (Christmas) surprise.

I was immediately sent back to the troop first aid station. That was still 2 km. But I managed. Beaming, I arrived there and received an envious congratulations from the medic. I had literally left everything behind. Only my wallet with the last letters and the Bible I had with me! At first, I was annoyed about it. But now I'm glad. Because on the way everything would have been taken from me. Maybe the company will send some of it home.

On the same day (on the 23rd) I reached the main first aid station and from there the field hospital, from which I wrote the airmail letter (No. 20) to you on the 25th.

However, as a wounded man, I still had to endure terrible hardships. On the 26th and 27th, the hospital was bombarded by Russians in rolling attacks, which, as we were helplessly exposed to the entire moral effect, completely wore down my last nerve strength. A bomb fell into the next room and was - a dud(!). I was relieved when we finally left on the 27th. However, not in an ambulance, but on open trucks. Here I had to endure terrible torment. Hardly anything to eat, poorest care, appalling conditions at the collection points. In addition, I froze both my feet to first degree. What hadn't happened in three weeks of living in a hole now happened after the injury.

After an adventurous journey, I was then loaded into a makeshift hospital train (freight car with beds) in Schachtz (80 km from Rostov) on the 30th. Here I spent New Year's Eve and New Year's Day, characterized by a thin punch, served at 2 am in Rostov.

They transported us a few hundred km back and unloaded us on the evening of the 2nd. Where I am now, I don't exactly know. Anyway, I was relieved that the train journey was over because the greatest blessing awaited me: Delousing!! Oh, what a feeling! As I lay under the shower, I literally possessed nothing more than my valuables. And then it was into white beds!

Since then, noteworthy things have happened again: My illnesses increase with the square of the distance from the front. On the way, I froze my feet, and in the hospital, I got jaundice. That bothers me the most now. My jaundice is only very mild. Most of all, I'm annoyed that I have no appetite. Because there are many long-missed things here. On the whole, though, I'm doing well. I'm enjoying the hygienic life to the fullest and, above all, have the happy awareness of being out of the "Battle in the Don Bend" (Schlacht im Donbogen). You can only guess what that means. Later I can tell you about it.

You will now want to know above all how the prospects are of getting home. Well, it does require quite a bit of luck. Conversely, the possibility still exists. The wounded are always transported from the front to this area and receive their first proper treatment or operation in field hospitals. When a new batch comes, the field hospitals have to be cleared again. Since I am fit to be transported, I certainly have the chance to go along. The question is just where such a train would go. That is then a matter of luck. After all, my replacement battalion is currently in Bautzen, a circumstance that might somehow be advantageous at some point.

Regardless of how it turns out: I can endure it here as well and am already infinitely grateful to have it this way. Anyway, I will do more than ever to hold the position as long as possible.

I just got - it's now the 7th - black tea again. Before that, there was honey and a cup of whole milk. A dream come true: honey milk! I will write more soon.

Yours sincerely, Walter

February 6, 1943*

Dear Loved Ones,

I've arrived at Grünberg in Silesia, within 24 hours. I'll provide more details tomorrow. The situation here is not bad. Mutti, you can slowly start preparing for a visit.

Yours affectionately,

Walter

> *When marked with an asterisk*, the text is translated directly from the original letter. The other excerpts are based on a printout (dated May 8, 1996) of Stephen Trobisch's translation of his father's letters which Walter's close friend Wolfgang Caffier had transcribed.*

THE FALL OF STALINGRAD: THE TANGANYIKA STANDARD (FEBRUARY 2, 1943)

[While Walter was recovering from the injuries he sustained at the Battle for Stalingrad, Ralph Hult was reading about the events in Dar es Salaam. The original Newspaper was found in a box containing Ralph Hult's last letter home. He died March 18, 1943 in Dar es Salaam.]

FIELD MARSHAL AND 16 GENERALS CAPTURED

Nazis Admit Southern Group of Sixth Army "Overwhelmed"

Moscow, February 1. A special Moscow announcement reports that the liquidation of the Axis troops in the western part of the centre of Stalingrad is complete. The German General Paulus (Hitler promoted him Field Marshal yesterday), Commander of his staff, including 16 generals, have been captured.

The Soviet midnight communique reports the occupation on the Trans-Caucasian front of the district centre and railway junction of Belorechenskaya and the district centres of Goryachy, Klyue and Ryszanskaya.

 Soviet forces on the North Caucasian, Voronezh, South-western, Leningrad and Volkhov fronts continued their offensive.

THE ARMY THAT INVADED BELGIUM

Moscow, Feb. 1 - Moscow Radio today reminded listeners that the Sixth German army, now destroyed at Stalingrad, was the army which smashed the Belgian defenses and invaded Belgium at the beginning of the war. – Reuter.

GUERILLA SUCCESS

Guerillas operating in the Orel region derailed three German military trains.

West of Voronezh, Soviet troops captured 20 inhabited localities and two railway stations.

AS BEFORE

Today's Moscow communique states "during the night of January 31 our troops on the south-western, southern and North Caucasian as well as on the Voronezh, Volkhov and Leningrad fronts continued offensive engagements against the enemy in same directions as before.

The German communique states: The southern group of the Sixth Army under Marshal Paulus has been overwhelmed.

The German Radio this afternoon announced "authoritatively" that the captured Marshal Paulus, commanding the trapped Stalingrad army has been "severely wounded while fighting with his groups." – Reuter.

> *The Tanganyika Standard. No. 3988. Dar Es Salaam, Tuesday, February 2 1943. Associated with The East African Standard and The Mombasa Times. First Article on the cover page.*

MUTTI'S SON WALTER WOUNDED A SECOND TIME (1943)

> *Walter was wounded three times. After his second injury in southern Russia - a gunshot fracture in his left upper arm - he was admitted to a hospital in Vienna on September 21, 1943.*
> *(Mutti)*

Vienna, September 22, 1943

Dear Loved Ones,

Mutti

By God's grace, I was once more rescued from a seemingly hope-less situation, this time through an injury. However, I was not spared this time - I received a penetrating gunshot to my left up-per arm. The bone was damaged, causing complete paralysis of the arm. They call this a "gunshot fracture." I can still move my fingers, a positive sign that the tendons are intact. The initial pain was almost unbearable, but since my arm has been cast in plaster, it's become manageable as long as I avoid awkward movements. I endure all of this with deep gratitude, seeing it as a valuable yet burdensome gift, and I am truly happy at heart.

The situation with the Army reserve was unfortunate! The old cy-cle restarted: encirclement, rearguard, retreat at night, fight dur-ing the day. We initially had to set up 15 km east of Mariupol. All night, we searched for our unit, a company cobbled together from the remnants of two battalions. We then retreated a bit every night until we positioned ourselves within the city itself on the evening of the 9th. However, the next morning we had to hastily evacuate as the enemy had landed from the sea. We narrowly escaped be-ing cut off, running through a barrage of fire. I was hit by a rock on my shoulder, but otherwise, I was unharmed.

In the evening, we established a new position about 10 km west of M[ariupol]. and dug in. At dawn, the enemy was already there. Their first attack faltered, leading them to take cover in a strip of bushes and start picking us off with snipers. The comrade with whom I shared a trench was hit in the head and fell unconscious. Despite the grim outlook, I hastily bandaged him. After a quarter of an hour, he regained consciousness. During this, I had man-aged to call a medic over. The medic then climbed into the trench with me for protection, and shortly after, I was hit. My chin and right cheek started to bleed but the medic bandaged me immedi-ately. It was then I noticed that I'd lost control of my left arm - it hung lifelessly. Pain started coursing through my upper arm. The only thought in my mind was to get away because the Russians could arrive at any moment. So, I decided against waiting for a proper bandaging, braced my left arm as best as I could, and started to move. I wanted to get straight to the battalion, a dangerous 200 m run across open terrain under sniper fire. It's a mystery how I managed to do it, but I did. My arm was bandaged, and I was given a shot of morphine to manage the pain. The final ordeal was a 5 km trek to the regiment's command post. I would have likely collapsed without the morphine.

I was then transported in an ambulance to the main medical station. The journey was filled with trials and tribulations. After a 150 km car journey, we reached a collection point for the wounded where I spent the following Sunday. We were loaded up on Monday and arrived in Zaporozhye on Tuesday morning in a cattle car filled with straw. I spent one night there in a field hospital where I received a plaster cast around my chest and arm. On Wednesday evening, I was fortunate to be loaded onto a proper hospital train which took us straight to Vienna as Lviv and Krakow were overcrowded. As I later learned, it was the last hospital train to leave Zaporozhye.

And now I am in Vienna! I have heard that I am in the best Vienna hospital (Reserve Hospital VIII b, 17, Dornbacherstr. 20). So far, my experiences have confirmed this. The best part is that instead of German Red Cross nurses, there are Catholic professional sisters here - it's a remarkable difference! Upon arrival, I was bathed wonderfully. My plaster cast has been recently changed. It looks somewhat daunting as my chest also needs to be in plaster to provide support to my arm. My upper arm has a significant bend to it. I expect to be here until Christmas, but I am able to stand, and I'm sure I won't be bored in Vienna. The fragments in my chin prevent me from shaving, so I am currently sporting a full U-boat beard. There are probably splinters in my arm too as several were visible in the x-ray.

Mutti

Finally, I am able to reconnect with you! I received no mail this time, so as you can imagine, I am eager to hear any news. Please resend any mail that was returned to you!

In terms of possessions, I am quite poor once more as I was left with nothing. However, we have been assured that we will receive everything from the women's organization. For now, could you please send me a few handkerchiefs and some writing paper? The ones I have currently are borrowed. I would also like to have my fountain pen along with some ink and refills. I never received any money either. I left with 2.50 M and that's all I have now. Could you also send me 100 M as soon as possible? Otherwise, I have everything I need. Are the apples ripe yet? I have a huge appetite for fruit and the food here seems excellent. We have an elevator to move from floor to floor, running hot and cold water in the room, where six of us are staying, and a view of the city. In a word: I am very satisfied here. Now, I eagerly await your letters.

Sending you warm greetings,

Your Walter

> *Translated from a computer printout of Walter's German letters, which is dated May 8, 1996, and was almost certainly made by Stephen Trobisch. Based on a transcription prepared by Wolfgang Caffier.*

Mamita

Final Thoughts

Ralph and I cherished a happy home. Our shared spiritual interests kept us connected, with God always at the forefront of our household. We were filled with joy over our children. As Paul, John, and Ingrid excelled in school, we knew we wanted to expand our family further. When Carl, our sixth child, was born, the doctor suggested methods to prevent more children, but we did not follow his advice. And when Gustav came along, my mother expressed that we had enough. Her comment angered me, and I replied with a rather sassy letter, as I still wasn't convinced that our family was complete. How about the rest of you? Isn't having sisters like Martha and Mary and brothers like Gustav and David wonderful?

As some of you may recall, there was one conflict in our home. Ralph grew up in a household where everything was done in an orderly manner. Even Mother Hult admitted that her husband was quite particular about this, which made it challenging for her to meet his standards, especially with eight children in the house. Ralph inherited this trait from his father. In my upbringing, such things were not as crucial. Mother was an exceptional cook, and we always had good food and enjoyable meals. She was a skilled seamstress, having trained as a dressmaker, so we had nice clothing, although not necessarily expensive. She was a hardworking woman and never lazy. Even in her 91st year, she remained mentally sharp and served as an inspiration. She would thoroughly clean the house every spring, including lifting and beating carpets, painting and wallpapering walls, and washing woodwork. However, she wasn't particular about putting everything away. Our living room table could be covered in papers and magazines, and it wasn't a top priority to tidy it up every day.

Consequently, I grew up without strictly adhering to the rule, "A place for everything and everything in its place." Thus, it was challenging to meet Ralph's standards, which greatly discouraged him. It also made me unhappy at times because I deeply loved him and wanted to please and make him happy. I tried my best and yearned for our home to be a model household, but I know it never quite reached that level in terms of tidiness, at least. And when we lived in such a small house, bursting with children, finding a place for everything was incredibly difficult. There were only a few dressers and one closet, so organizing belongings was a constant challenge.

Our home was built on numerous joyful elements, with the cornerstone being Jesus Christ and our unwavering faith in Him.

Our intimate life was temperate yet always mutually satisfying and happy. No matter what the storms of life, they only drew us closer to one another.

In my youth, I learned, "You did not choose me, but I chose you and appointed you, that you should go and bear fruit and that your fruit should abide, so that whatever you ask the Father in my name, He may give it to you" (John 15:16).

I raise my Ebenezer here and declare, "Hitherto hath the Lord helped." I entrust Him to each of my sons and daughters and any future sons and daughters who will join our family. I also extend this trust to my grandchildren and those yet to come.

May the divine spark illuminating this mortal existence touch your hearts and lives, inspiring you to bring glory to Him! Remember, He cares for you!

"Therefore, my beloved brethren, whom I love and long for, my joy and crown, stand firm thus in the Lord, my beloved... Rejoice in the Lord always; again, I say, rejoice" (Philippians 4:1.4).

Mamita

As your mother and grandmother, Gertrude Leona Jacobson Hult, I leave you with these heartfelt words. Remember to rejoice in the Lord, even amid challenges and trials, for He is with you every step of the way. May you always find strength and joy in your faith, holding steadfast to the teachings of the Lord.

With love and blessings,

Gertrude Leona Jacobson Hult

EPILOGUE

Mamita and Mutti's narratives conclude before they meet for the first time at their children's wedding in Germany. After the passing of Ralph, Mamita moves to Bolivia in 1947, dedicating herself to work at an orphanage, Bible School, and Christian bookstore. Meanwhile, Mutti faces her own challenges after losing her husband Martin in 1957. A year later, she embarks on a new chapter in Africa, residing with Walter and Ingrid in Cameroon while teaching German at a high school. Eventually, her health declines, leading her to move with Walter and Ingrid to Austria, where she passes away in 1966 at age 73 and is buried in the town of Attersee.

As for Mamita, after returning from Bolivia in 1960, her life journey continues through Springfield, Missouri, and Minneapolis before her passing in 1991 at age 92. She finds her final resting place in Colona, Illinois, with a tombstone inscription that reads:

Gertrude Leona (Jacobson) Hult
Wife of Pastor Ralph D. Hult (1888-1943)
The pioneer missionary to Africa from the Augustana Lutheran
Church. He is buried in Dar es Salaam, Tanzania.
Mother of Paul, Ruth, John, Ingrid, Veda, Eunice, Carl, Martha,
Gustav, Mary, and David.
Missionary in Bolivia between 1947 and 1960. During her later years,
she was lovingly known as 'Mamita' as she was called by the children
she cared for in a Bolivian orphanage.
(Col. 3:17) [And whatsoever ye do in word or deed, do all in the name
of the Lord Jesus, giving thanks to God and the Father by him.]

MAMITA AND MUTTI MEET FOR THE FIRST TIME (1952)

Walter and I arrived at Pastor Fuchs's home late that evening after a ride on the familiar Trobisch motorcycle—a ride that stirred memories. On the door was a large hand-lettered sign: "HERZLICH WILLKOMMEN" painted across a map of Africa. I must have looked as though I had ridden straight from the Dark Continent. The cold cream I had put on my face as protection against the wind and sun served as an excellent dust collector while we sped through villages and along country roads.

We rang the doorbell. Who was the first to throw her arms about me but Mother! This was our first meeting in five years. And then followed the warm embrace of brother John. I had come just in time, for in a few days he and Louise would have to return to the States from Germany, his term as an army doctor at an end. None of my other brothers and sisters could be here for this reunion. But there were "Mutti" and "Vati," Walter's mother and father, who had just arrived from the Russian Zone. These were indeed the sweet fruits of waiting—to be once more united, coming as we did from the far places of the globe.

Then the busy time that followed. A few days later Walter wrote in our journal: Here I am once more at the 'Standesamt,' the German office for the civil marriage required by law. This has taken a lot of time, and a lot of paper, and has cost a lot of money. Every official paper Ingrid sent me from Africa had to have two translations, because she was in French territory and the papers were in English.

"And the questions they've asked me here:

"'Where was your fiancé born?' — 'In Tanzania.'

"'Which part of Germany is that?' — 'It's in Africa.'

Epilogue

"'Is she a native?' — 'No, she's an American.'

"'Of what descent?' — 'Swedish.'

"'Where is her mother?' — 'In Bolivia, South America.'

"'What's her name?' — 'Gertrude L. Hult.'

"'What does the L. stand for?' — 'I don't know.'

"'Then you can't get your marriage license until you find out. In Germany no initial letters are permitted.'"

June 2 was the day of full surrender — each for the other — both for Christ!

We began the day's celebration with a festive dinner for our family and out-of-town guests. Those two hours were rich and memorable. There were toasts in honor of the occasion, table songs (Mutti wrote a classic in German, French, and English, relating the whole story of the Hult-Trobisch romance), and music by the Fuchs family. Most moving of all was the toast given by Walter's father. (It had been more difficult for Mutti and Vati to get a pass from the authorities of East Germany to attend their son's wedding than for me to come from another continent.) For the benefit of the new relatives from across the sea, Vati reviewed briefly his son's turbulent life to date.

We were thankful to be able to have our wedding in the beautiful and reverent atmosphere of the Christuskirche, the only large Protestant church in Mannheim not damaged by bombs.

> *Ingrid Trobisch, On Our Way Rejoicing (Quiet Waters Publications: Bolivar, Missouri, 2000). [Earlier editions by other publishers 1964, 1973, 1976.]*

MUTTI ARRIVES IN AFRICA (1958)

On August 12, 1958, at 5:20 pm, the aircraft takes off from Berlin-Tempelhof Airport. In just fifteen minutes, we have ascended above the clouds, the sun now gleaming brightly above us. Our flight to Frankfurt proceeds at an elevation of 3,000 meters. No sooner have we relaxed and unfastened our seatbelts, when a voice comes over the loudspeaker, instructing us to re-buckle. Suddenly, we find ourselves amidst a thunderstorm. Rain cascades down on the exterior of the plane, and we experience significant turbulence, with the aircraft being thrown about. Fortunately, this discomfort only lasts for a brief period, and after we make it through, dinner is served. The sandwiches are conveniently stowed in the front seat pocket. They are made with white bread, filled with salmon, ham, sausage, and cheese, accompanied by lemon juice, a fruit bowl, and a slice of cake. As we prepare to land, we are treated to a breathtaking view of the river Main and Frankfurt. We land at 7:00 pm.

Upon landing, passport checks are conducted swiftly. All passengers intending to travel abroad are guided into a separate room. It's a large room, amply illuminated by the abundant windows and glass doors. However, we are completely isolated from the world beyond this room. I eagerly search for Klaus and Inge [Mutti's son and daughter-in-law] through the windows, but to no avail. Suddenly, behind me, I hear Klaus' distinctive whistle! Inge has found me against all odds. As we try to make ourselves comfortable in a corner, a control officer tells Inge that she misunderstood, she's not allowed to be in this room. After a lot of persuasion, he finally concedes to let us converse near him. There's not much time left anyway, as at 7:40 pm, the same plane departs for Paris. As we rise into the air, I take in the sights of the river Main and the Taunus mountains. The aircraft ascends rapidly, causing an earache, which doesn't subside until we arrive in Paris.

Epilogue

I have no view from the plane until we approach Paris, where the endless city lights sprawl beneath us, seeming to move towards us rapidly. We land at Paris airport at 9:30 pm.

It's 6:00 am when I disembark in Douala, setting foot on African soil for the first time. A warm, humid air surrounds me. Not long after, a fierce thunderstorm breaks out, with rainfall unlike anything I've ever experienced before. "A Douala, il pleut toujours," comments the French woman who was my seatmate during the night flight. About half an hour later, she must brave the downpour to catch her onward flight to Brazzaville.

This moist weather prevails for the four weeks that I stay in Elat. Light rain falls occasionally, but it's far from sufficient to relieve the severe drought or to wash away the red dust from the bushes and mountains. The locals don't refer to these light showers as rain but dew.

In a predictable pattern, daylight breaks at 6:00 am and dusk falls at 6:00 pm, both transitions happening very swiftly. By 7:00, it's either bright as day or pitch black. The sun rarely shines brightly, but even its subdued presence at noon generates enough heat to make staying indoors preferable. Yet, at night, the temperature drops sufficiently that a blanket becomes desirable in the early morning hours.

The slightest breeze brings welcome relief from the heat. Here in Elat, we're surrounded by a mountainous landscape. The peaks that encircle the wide, relatively flat valley where Elat lies, at an altitude of about 1,000 meters, are forested up to the top.

The road that extends from Yaoundé to Elat-Ebolowa cuts directly through the jungle. On both sides, the dense underbrush and trees are so thick that they would be unnavigable for a European. Besides, the road doesn't match my previous mental image of African roads. Instead of the flat, dull paths crossing an endless plain that I'd envisaged, these roads resemble hilly terrain that is rarely

197

flat, winding across many valleys and heights, and offer surprisingly beautiful vistas where the jungle has been partially cleared.

Two types of giant trees lining the road particularly captivate me. One is a giant palm, its fronds rustling in the wind, simulating rainfall, and the other is a true acacia with genuine acacia leaves and stunning, large, full, golden-yellow clusters. Near the settlements, which consist of simple mud huts arranged in a sort of linear village on either side of the road, there are also banana trees, their fruit hanging in heavy clusters, alongside plantain trees, whose fruit resembles green bananas and is eaten as a vegetable. The lemon, orange, and grapefruit trees here bear a resemblance to the largest apple trees in Germany, although the fruits are small and often fall off unripe, with the exception of the grapefruits. Large cocoa plantations are also present; the cocoa bush here is about the height of a man.

Upon my return to Libamba, I discover something new every day, and I document these observations as they come, in a vibrant mix. In the flower garden, I find marigolds, geraniums thriving in the flower box, and tall climbing roses swaying in the wind by the house. Their clusters of flowers are so sparse that they remind me of vetch. In his vegetable garden, Walter grows beans, spinach, beetroot, cucumbers, tomatoes, and lettuce. Pineapple plants reach up towards the sun with their pink fruits, which take about a year to ripen. Around the garden, a raspberry hedge grows, its fruits are a hybrid in taste and appearance of raspberries and wild strawberries back home.

Everywhere, bindweed grows robustly, its white or purple flowers are giant versions of the modest ones in Germany. The garden demands a lot of care, often employing two boys. When it doesn't rain, watering needs to be done in the morning and evening. After heavy rain showers, the soil needs immediate loosening through hoeing. Whenever the sun shines, lettuce needs to be shaded with palm fronds. New seed beds are covered with grass to retain soil condition and prevent minerals from washing away too easily. This is why the locals change their gardens annually.

In terms of domestic animals, in addition to cats and rather small dogs, I observe chickens, geese, ducks, goats, and pigs. The goats and pigs are consistently smaller than their European counterparts.

Translated from Mutti's handwritten notes.

MAMITA TO DAUGHTER VEDA (1949 AND 1959)

La Paz, Bolivia, December 1, 1949

Dearest Veda,

I've been meaning to write to you for a while now, but somehow, I never quite manage to sit down and do so. I trust this letter finds you in good health and high spirits. Your letter, received months ago, filled me with joy. Please, won't you write again?

I continue to find fulfillment in my role as matron of the Mission Home. Are you a subscriber to our church's paper, the "Vision"? If not, I believe you would genuinely enjoy it.

I am pleased to share that I have met all the Spanish language requirements and successfully passed all the exams set by our language committee. This achievement is usually expected within the first two years on the field. I am indeed grateful for the opportunity to carry out such meaningful work here.

Do take a moment to write back and fill me in on your own adventures, as well as updates about your brothers and so forth.

With much love,

Epilogue

Gertrude Hult

La Paz, Bolivia, December 6, 1959

Dearest Veda,

During the holiday season, we make an effort to send letters to our dear ones. I often find myself thinking of you and wishing we could see each other more often. Regrettably, I don't often sit down to pen a letter. Whenever I do hear from you, it's always a delight, and I am eagerly awaiting your Christmas letter. When I finally make the trip home, I will make it a priority to visit you. At this point, however, I'm not sure when that will be.

Currently, I'm based in La Paz. At the end of the Bible school year, I volunteered to act as matron of the Mission Home during the holiday break. However, they wanted me to return to the Bible School. As a result, I informed the Executive Committee that I was open to being placed either at the Bible School or the Mission Home. To my surprise, I was assigned to neither but to the branch bookstore situated in the Indian town.

Meanwhile, Ingrid and Walter are in Libamba, where Walter teaches at a Christian college. His mother also teaches there—she instructs in German. They are looking forward to the arrival of their fourth child, expected in January.

Much love,

Gertrude Hult

> *Excerpts from two letters in the possession of Gus Hult, Mamita's son.*

Epilogue

MAMITA AND MUTTI MEET AGAIN IN
LIBAMBA, CAMEROON (CA. 1962)

Now I had two grandmothers in Libamba. My grandmother from Germany had been with us ever since I was born. She helped my father in the school and taught classes for the Africans because she was a teacher. And now, my grandmother from America was with us, too.

Although I was very happy to have two grandmothers taking care of me, it sometimes made my day more difficult. Because when I said to my mother in the morning, "Will Grandmother pick me up from kindergarten today?" she would always say "Yes."

But I never knew who would come and walk home with me. Sometimes, my German grandmother came, sometimes, my American grandmother came; one day, both of them came, and one day, no one came, and I had to walk home alone.

"We will have to find a better solution," I thought in my big, four-cornered head.

So, I asked my American grandmother, "What is your first name, Grandma?"

"Gertrude," she said.

"Do you mind if I call you Grandma Gertrude, then?" I asked.

"Oh, no. Not at all," she answered.

And then, I asked my German grandmother, "What is your first name?"

201

Epilogue

"Gertrude, as well," she said and laughed. "Only a true Pumpel-hoober has two grandmothers with the same first name."

But the next day, I had another idea. "Grandma, where is your real home?" I asked my American grandmother.

"My real home is in Springfield, Missouri. That's where your Mommy grew up. It's in North America."

"But why did you go to La Paz in South America?" I wanted to know.

"You see, Pumpelhoober, in La Paz, there were many children who had no mother or father. They are called orphans, and when I heard that they needed someone who could take care of them, I wrote to the mission director and asked him if I could go there. I thought, even though I'm already a grandmother, I could still be like a mother to those children. The mission director was very happy that someone wanted to take care of them, so I went to Bo-livia. I've been there for many years."

Then, I had a brilliant idea. I asked her, "Did the children in Bo-livia call you 'Grandma,' as I do?"

"No, in Bolivia, they speak Spanish. They called me 'Mamita.' That means 'little mother.'"

"May I call you 'Mamita' as well?" I wanted to know.

Grandma nodded.

Then, I asked my German grandmother, "What is 'little mother' in German?"

Epilogue

"Mu-tti," she said, and she pronounced it with a long 'oo' as in 'food', 'Mutti.'

"Do you mind if I call you 'Mutti,' then?"

"Oh no, not at all."

So that is what everyone did from then on. We called my American grandmother 'Mamita,' and we called my German grandmother 'Mutti.' And, never again, did I have to walk home alone from kindergarten.

> *David Trobisch, The Adventures of Pumpelhoober in Africa America and Germany (Bolivar, Missouri: Quiet Waters Publications, 2001) First Edition: 1968.*

TABLE OF DOCUMENTS

Coal Mining in Illinois (1867) 14

Brothers Ernst Friedrich and Gottlob Heinrich Pfitzer of
Oschatz (1845-1902) 30

Ralph Hult and Gertrude Jacobson Meet (1917) 46

Sudan United Mission and Dr. Karl Kumm (1902) 49

Ralph Hult about Karl Kumm (1917) 51

Ralph Hult Asking for Gertrude Jacobson's Hand
(9/20/1917) 56

Wedding of Ralph and Gertrude Hult (7/9/1919) 89

Mamita's Journal of Paul's Babyhood (1921-1922) 106

Conflicts Between the Mission Board and the Sudan
United Mission 113

The Sorbian Nation 116

Coat of Arms Trobisch Family (1640-1888) 119

Mamita's Grandparents Visit In Verona (1929) 142

Leipzig Windscheidstrasse (1928) 147

Sinking of the Zam Zam (Ralph Hult, 1941) 152

Ralph Hult's Last Letter to Mamita (March 4-6, 1943) 158

Mamita Receives the News of Ralph Hult's Death (March
18, 1943) 164

Biographical Dates - Ralph Daniel Hult 167

Letters from the Eastern Front (Stalingrad 1942/43) 172

Epilogue

The Fall of Stalingrad: The Tanganyika Standard
(February 2, 1943)..183

Mutti's Son Walter Wounded a Second Time (1943) 184

Mamita and Mutti meet for the first time (1952) 194

Mutti arrives in Africa (1958) 196

Mamita to Daughter Veda (1949 and 1959)................................199

Mamita and Mutti meet again in Libamba, Cameroon (ca.
1962)..201

Epilogue

BIBLIOGRAPHY

Eleanor Anderson, *Miracle at Sea: The Sinking of the Zamzam and Our Family's Rescue.* 2nd ed. (Bolivar, Missouri: Quiet Waters Publications, 2001). [Eleanor Anderson was one of the children in the boat with Ralph Hult when the Zamzam was sunk.]

John E. Hult, *Growing Up in the Ozarks.* (Bolivar, Missouri: Quiet Waters Publications 2001).

S. Hjalmar Swanson and Augustana Synod Mission. *Zamzam: The Story of a Strange Missionary Odyssey* (Board of Foreign Missions of the Augustana Synod 1944). [Reprint: Bolivar, Missouri: Quiet Waters Publications, 2007).

David Trobisch, *The Adventures of Pumpelhoober in Africa America and Germany* (Bolivar MO: Quiet Waters Publications 2001). [First English Edition: Concordia Pub. House 1971).]

Ingrid Trobisch, On Our Way Rejoicing (Bolivar, Missouri: Quiet Waters Publications, 2000). [Earlier editions by other publishers 1964, 1973, 1976.]

Maps

MAPS

Mamita's Manuscript

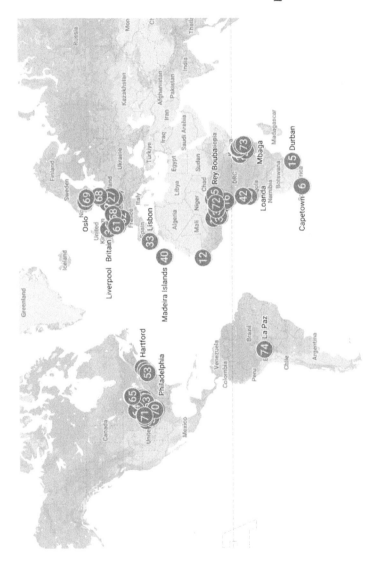

Maps

1. Axtell
2. Bethesda
3. Bielefeld
4. Bloomington
5. Cable
6. Capetown
7. Chicago
8. Cleveland
9. Colona
10. Copenhagen
11. Dahome
12. Dakar
13. Dar-es-salaam
14. Douala
15. Durban
16. Elat
17. Funk
18. Gardner
19. Garoua
20. Geneseo
21. Hamburg
22. Hartford
23. Hepburn
24. Ibi
25. Iramba
26. Leipzig
27. Berlin
28. Kewanee
29. Kona
30. Lagos
31. Ibi
32. Lindsborg
33. Lisbon
34. Liverpool
35. Loanda
36. Lokoja
37. London
38. Machame
39. Macomb
40. Madeira Islands
41. Mashame
42. Matadi
43. Mbaga
44. Moline
45. Moshi
46. New Sweden
47. New York
48. Numan
49. Omaha
50. Osceola
51. Oslo
52. Paris
53. Philadelphia
54. Rapid River
55. Rey Bouba
56. Rock Island
57. Rogersville
58. Rotterdam
59. Sherrard
60. Shigatini
61. Southampton
62. Springfield
63. St. David
64. St. Peter
65. Stonington
66. Swedeburg
67. Tanga
68. Tyrings
69. Varmland
70. Verona
71. Wahoo
72. Wukari
73. Zanzibar
74. La Paz
75. Rock Island

Maps

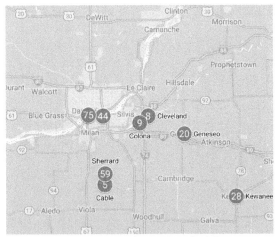

Geneseo / Springfield

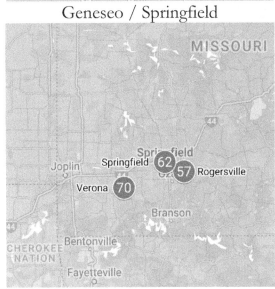

Maps

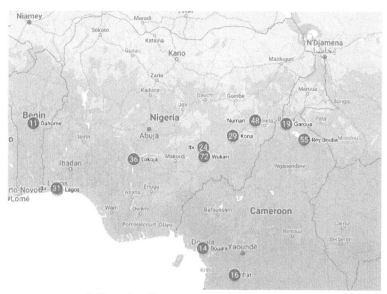

Nigeria Cameroon / Tanzania

Maps

Europe

Maps

Mutti's Manuscript

Maps

1. Bautzen
2. Berlin
3. Camburg
4. Diesbar
5. Eibenstock
6. Elstertal
7. Elstra
8. Finow
9. Grävenitz
10. Greiz
11. Jena
12. Jocketa
13. Kairlindach
14. Kamenz
15. Langenzenn
16. Leipzig
17. Liebau
18. Manebach
19. München
20. Neustadt
21. Niederkaina
22. Nünchritz
23. Oberschlema
24. Olbernhau
25. Plauen
26. Prietitz
27. Reichenbach
28. Riesa
29. Ruppertsgrün
30. Schmiedeberg
31. Stargard
32. Taubenheim
33. Wien
34. Ypern
35. Zempin

Maps

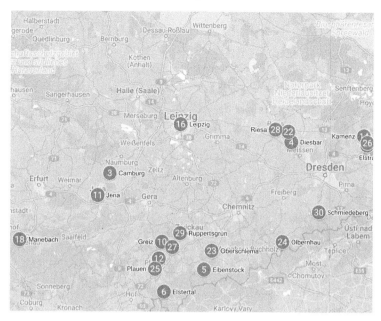

Leipzig / Bautzen

215

Notes

Made in the USA
Monee, IL
08 August 2023